Mel Bay Presents

CLASSICAL BANJO

arranged and adapted by Larry Vanek

Visit us on the Web at www.melbay.com — E-mail us at email@melbay.com

TABLE OF CONTENTS

TABLE OF CONTENTS (cont'd)

INTRODUCTION

The arrangements in this book are oriented but not limited to banjo players with a bluegrass background and three-finger right hand technique and assume a basic familiarity with certain techniques such as melodic style and single string style.

Since many banjo players find reading standard musical notation somewhat intimidating, I hoped to make the music in this book more accessible by transcribing it in tablature, with its added advantage of being able to provide chosen fingerings.

The arrangements assume an ability to read basic tablature along with a knowledge of time signatures and note values used in standard musical notation. Due to the rhythmic complexity of the music, I've incorporated time values into the tablature along with some standard symbolization and terminology. I've provided an explanation of my tablature system and most of the symbols and terminology used in the section that follows. Any symbols or terminology that are not dealt with in this section can be easily found in almost any basic music theory text. As opposed to most tablature, I've included right hand indications only in difficult passages where the preferred right hand technique might not be obvious.

In these transcriptions I've tried to adhere as closely as possible to the original music and what I perceived to be the original spirit or feeling of the music. Obviously, transcribing classical music for the five-string banjo presents many technical difficulties due to such characteristics of the instrument as limited range and lack of sustain. Due to these limitations it became necessary to accept the fact that certain pieces of music were simply not suitable for transcription.

I have played all of these arrangements extensively in an effort to ensure that all were playable for the intermediate to advanced player, and have made every effort to find what I felt to be the best fingerings for each individual piece. The player should also feel free to experiment with the fingerings or positions which are most comfortable for him or her.

As a final word, the music in this book is grouped by composer and arranged in chronological order rather than by degree of difficulty, as is the case in some collections. An idea of the relative difficulty of the individual works can be obtained from the introductions at the beginning of each section. Hopefully, this music will provide some new ways of looking at the fingerboard and open up some new musical perspectives.

Notation and Terminology Used in the Tablature

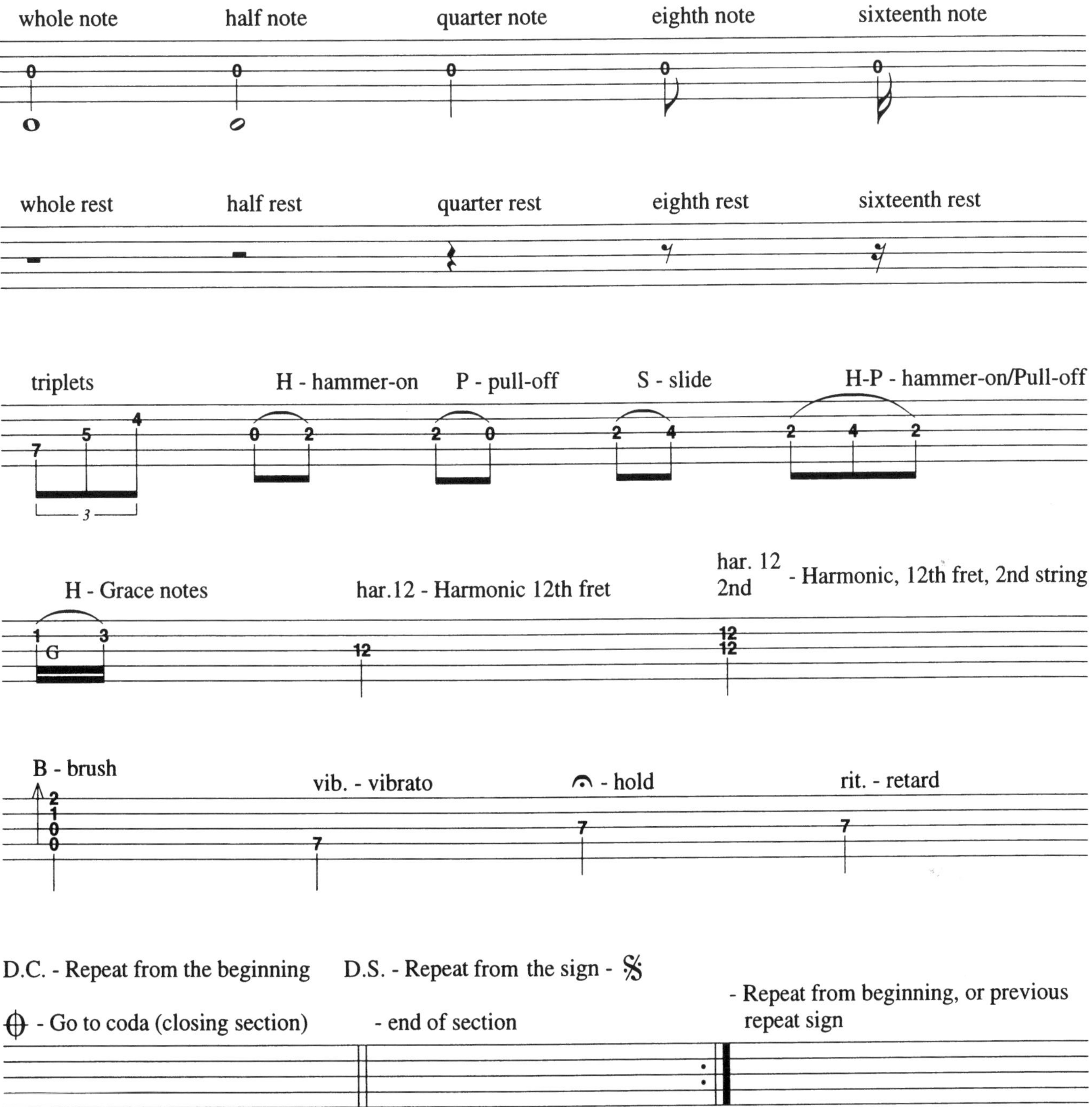

Grace note: A note whose time value is not counted in the general rhythm and must be subtracted from that of the preceding or following note.

Right hand indications:
T = Thumb
I = Index finger
2 = Second finger
L-M = Line-Measure: L15-M2 would refer to the second measure of the 15th line in a given piece of music.

C tuning (4th string down to C)

FIVE PIECES BY J.S. BACH (1685-1750)

Bourree in E Minor

Prelude No. 1 (from the "Well-Tempered Clavier")

Prelude from Cello Suite No. 1

Jesu, Joy of Man's Desiring

Invention No. 10 (for two banjos)

Bach's music is particularly well-suited to the banjo and "Bourree in E Minor" is no exception. This short, recognizable work should be played with a steady, balanced rhythm.

"Prelude No. 1," a medium length work, is from the "Well-Tempered Clavier," a collection of 48 preludes and fugues written in every key. This piece also falls in the intermediate category even though it too contains some fairly unorthodox right-hand technique in certain spots, notably L1 through L3 - M1, and the concluding measures. A good version of "Prelude No. 1" for classical guitar can be found on Christopher Parkening's "Christopher Parkening Plays Bach" album.

"Prelude from Cello Suite No. 1" is a piece that works beautifully on the banjo but is very demanding in technique. It extensively utilizes both melodic style and single string style and involves some fairly punishing left hand stretches. Due to the many difficult right hand passages, I have chosen to include right hand indications throughout the whole piece. Despite all this, it is one of my favorite pieces in this collection and, after being transposed from the original cello music in the key of G, remains very faithful to the original in terms of the intervals used. Of special interest is the use of a "blue" note (a minor third) in L19 - M1, and the chromatic passage that follows.

"Jesu, Joy of Man's Desiring" is a well known work that contains one of the most beautiful melodies ever written. Like "prelude from Cello Suite No. 1" it is extremely challenging but also offers great musical rewards. This work is in 3/4 time and it is essential that the flowing quality of the triplets in this time signature be retained, despite the technical difficulty of many passages. Therefore, it is strongly recommended that the player obtain a recording of this piece before attempting to play it. An excellent rendition of this work for classical guitar exists on Christopher Parkening's "Christopher Parkening Plays Bach."

"Invention No. 10" is transcribed for two banjos with the first banjo part constituting a complete solo in itself. I would place this piece in the intermediate range of difficulty, although some of the right hand technique gets a bit tricky due to the extensive use of the low D string, especially in the second banjo part.

BOURRÉE IN E MINOR

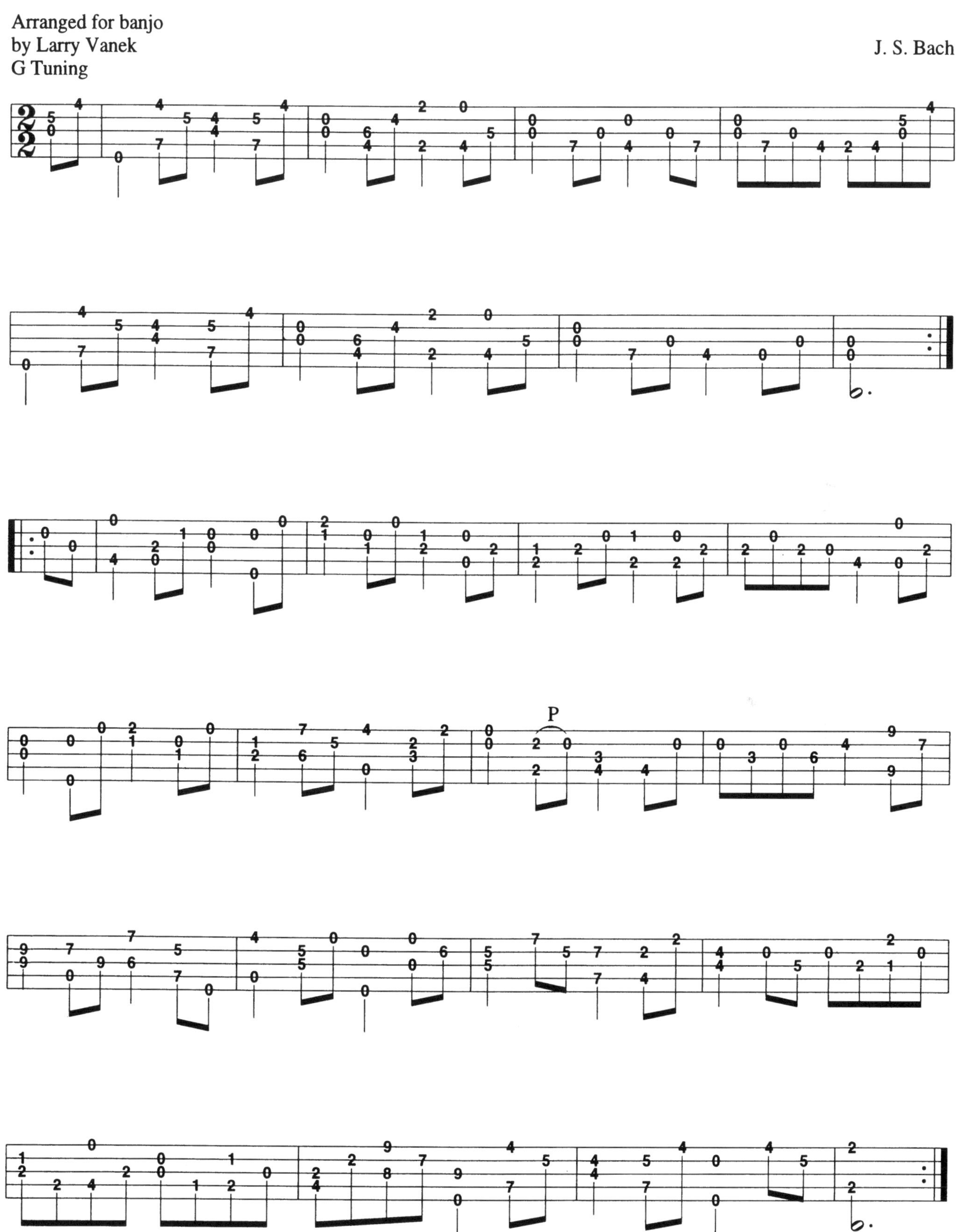

PRELUDE NO. 1

(from the Well-Tempered Clavier)

Arranged for banjo
by Larry Vanek
C Tuning

J.S. Bach

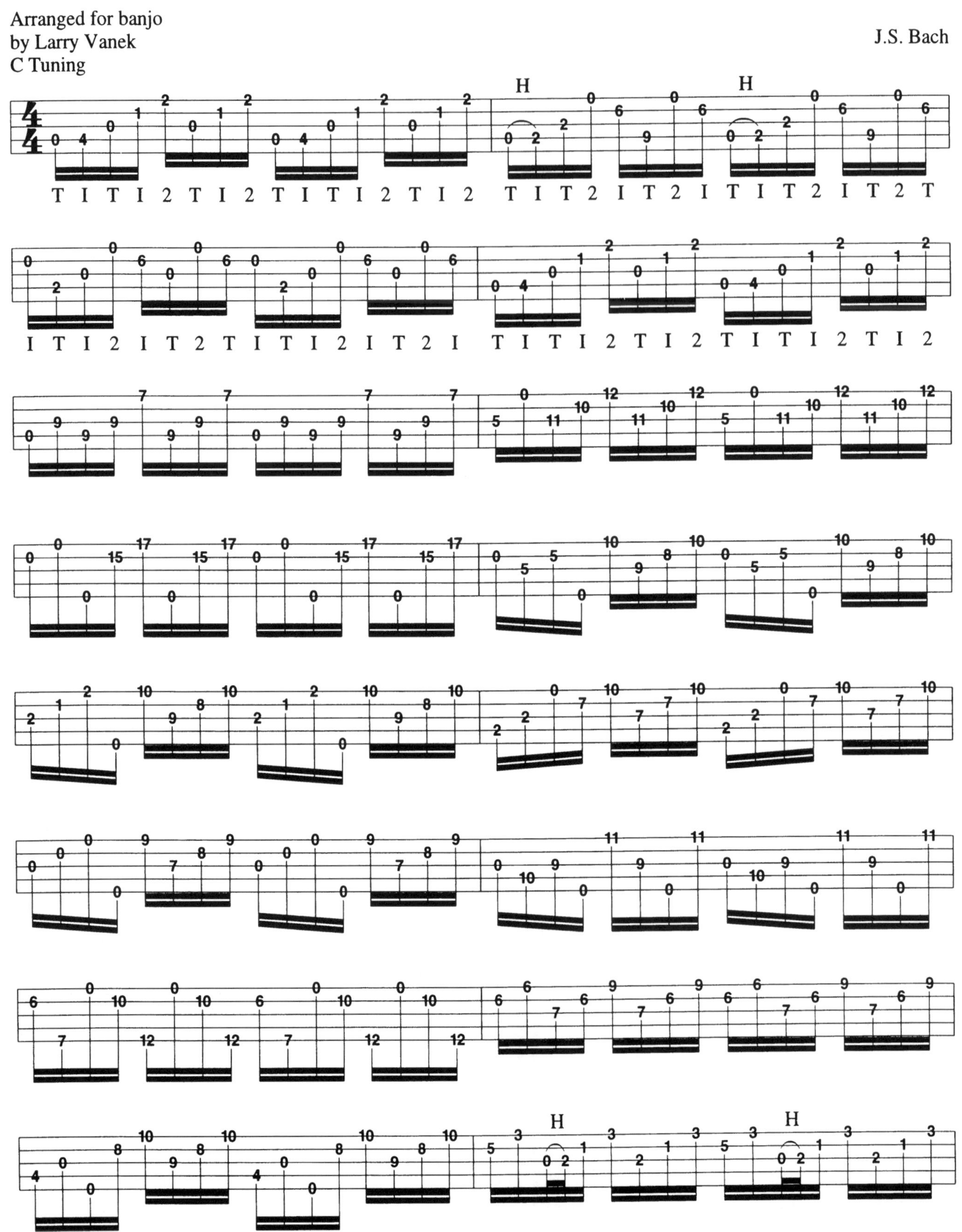

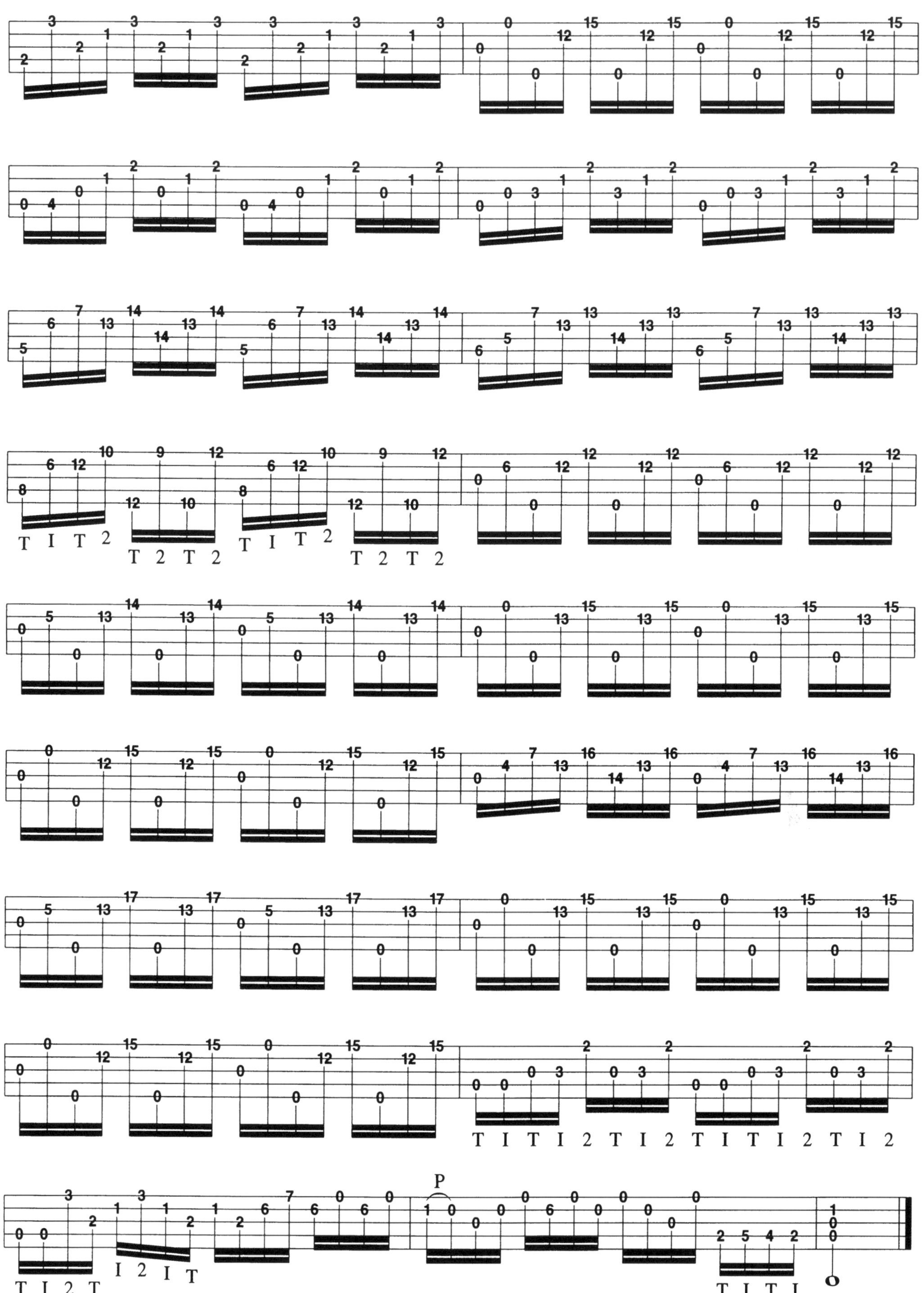
T I T 2 T 2 T 2 T I T 2 T 2 T 2
T I T I 2 T I 2 T I T I 2 T I 2
T I 2 T I 2 I T
P
T I T I

PRELUDE FROM CELLO SUITE NO. 1

Arranged for banjo
by Larry Vanek
C Tuning

J. S. Bach

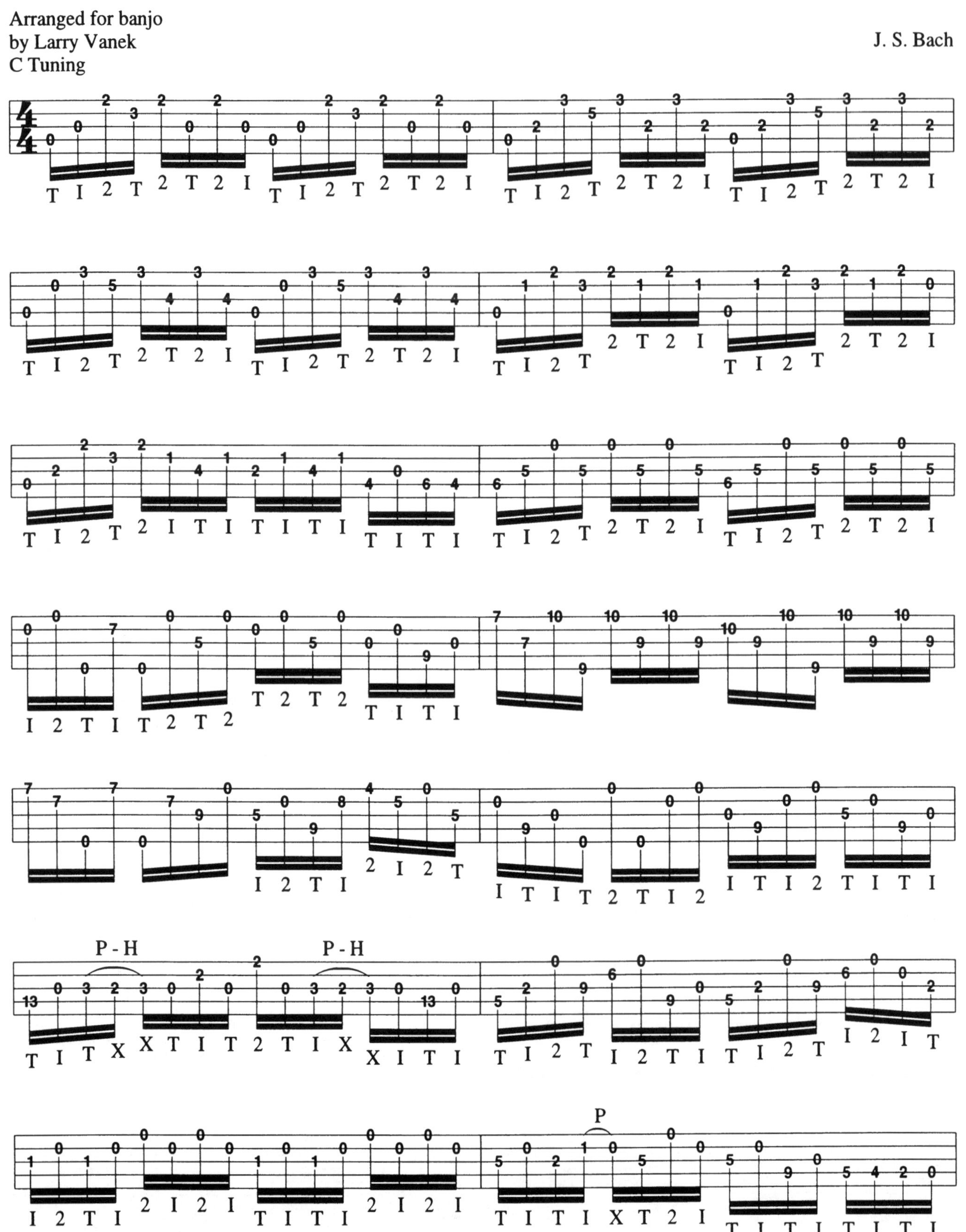

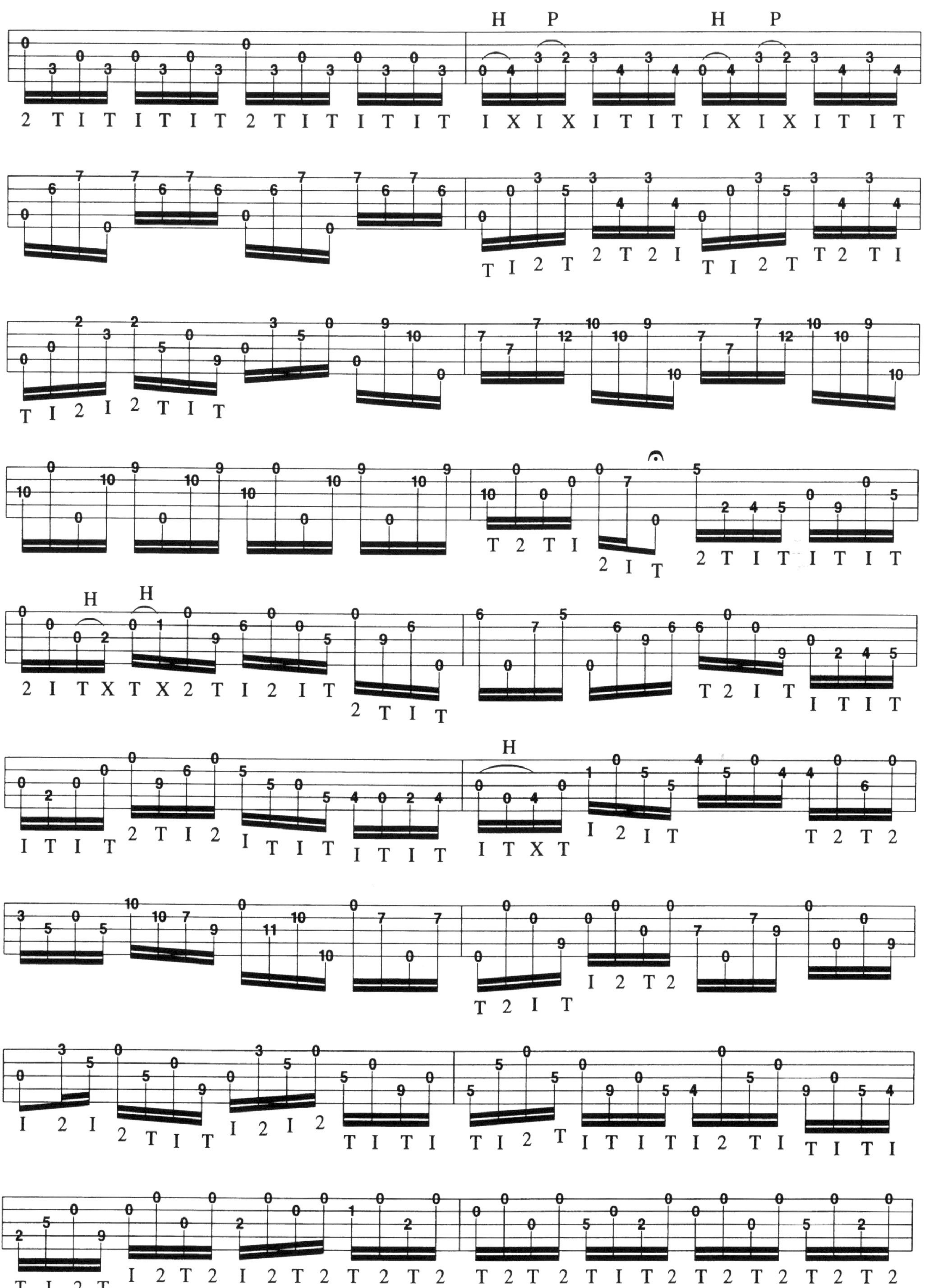

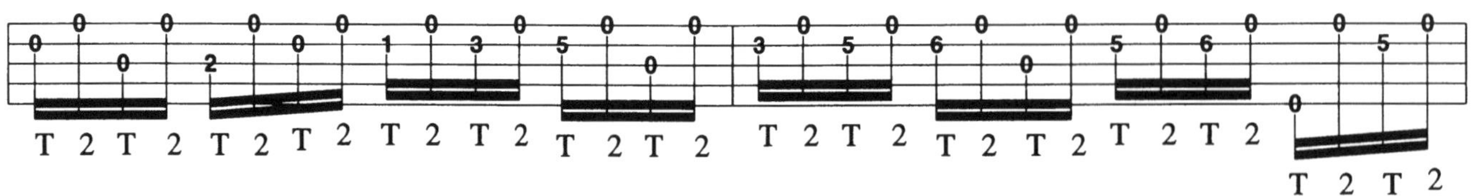

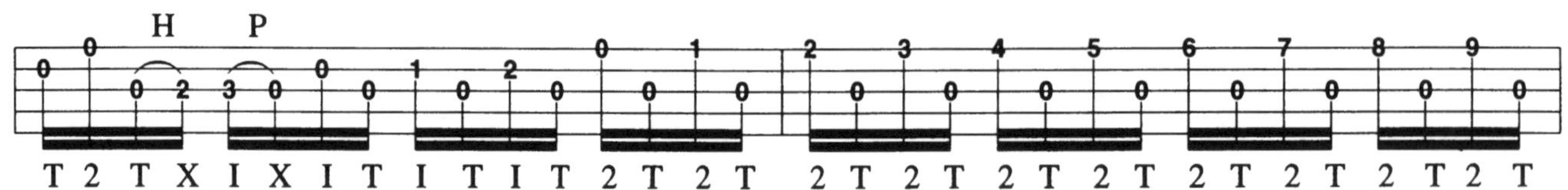

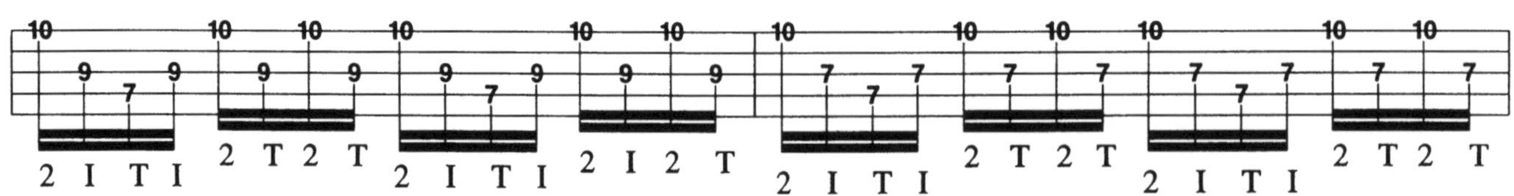

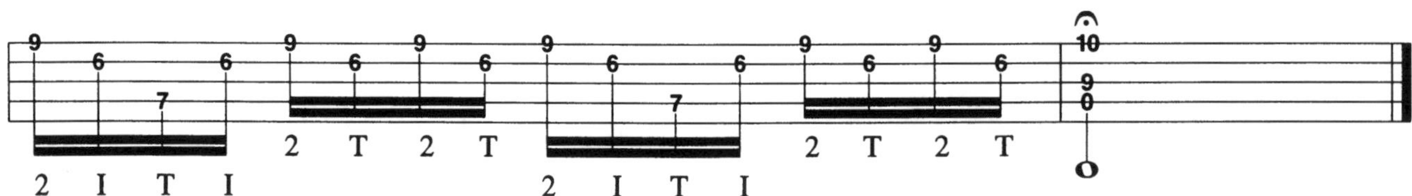

This page has been left blank to avoid awkward page turns

JESU, JOY OF MAN'S DESIRING

Arranged for banjo
by Larry Vanek
C Tuning

J. S. Bach

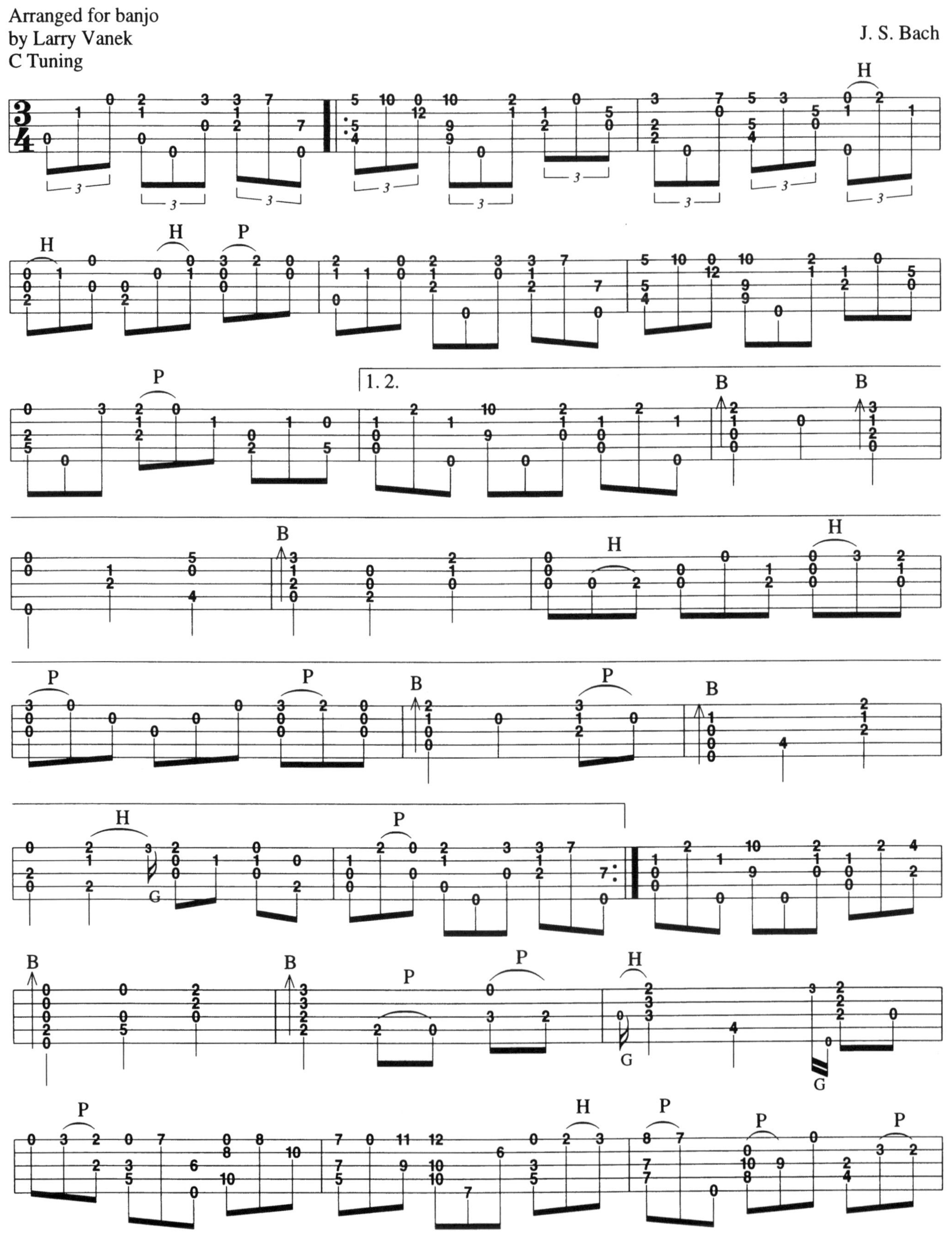

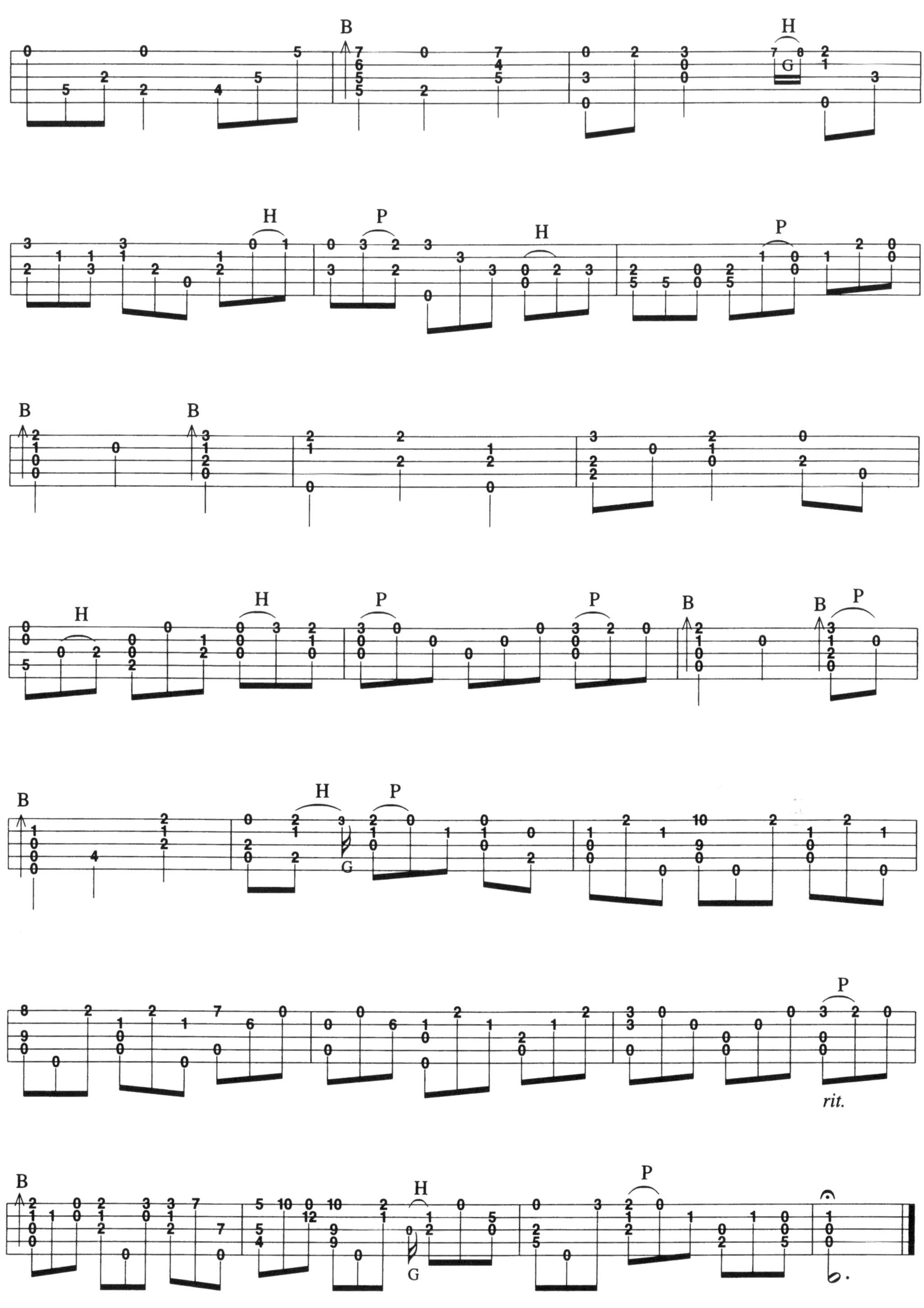
rit.

INVENTION NO. 10

Arranged for banjo
by Larry Vanek
G Tuning

J. S. Bach

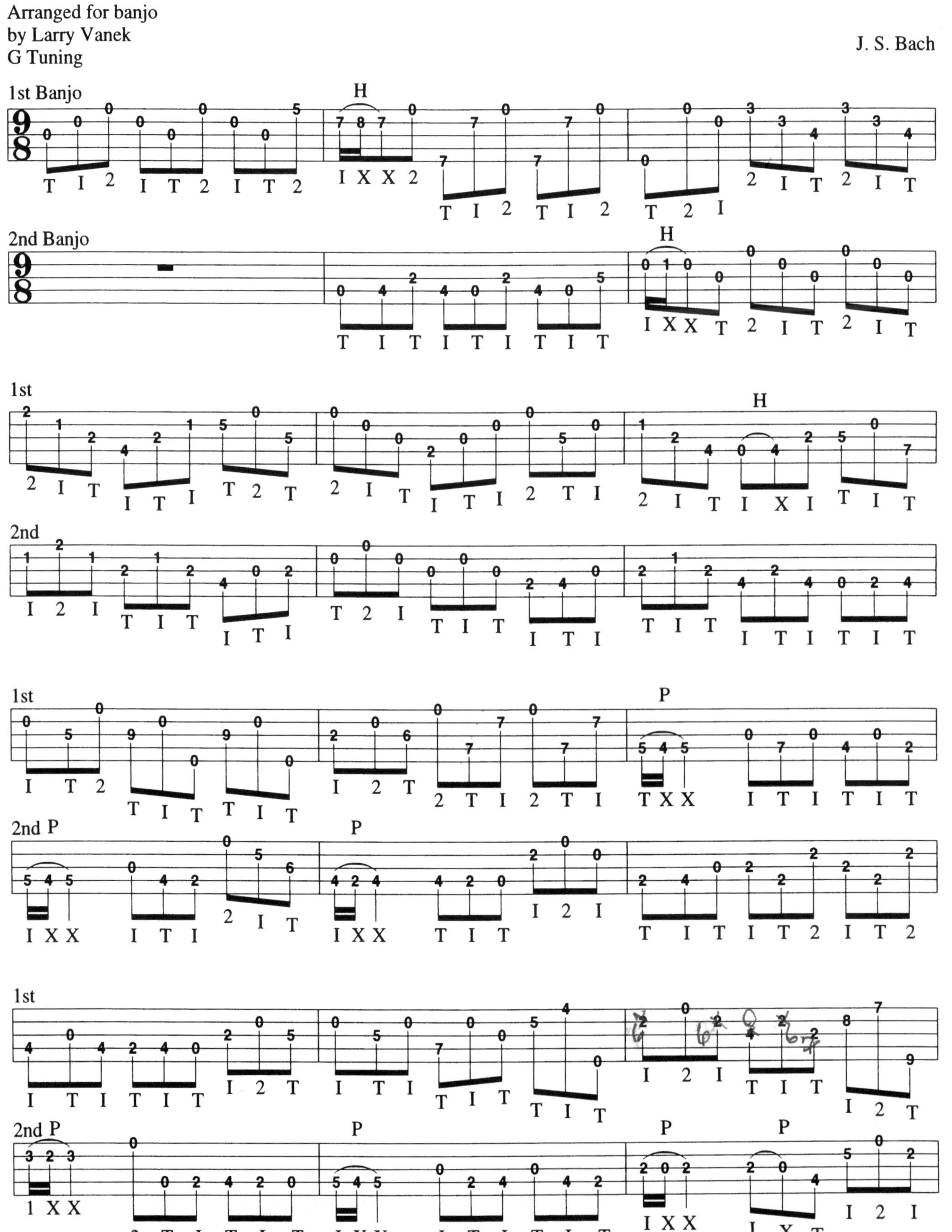

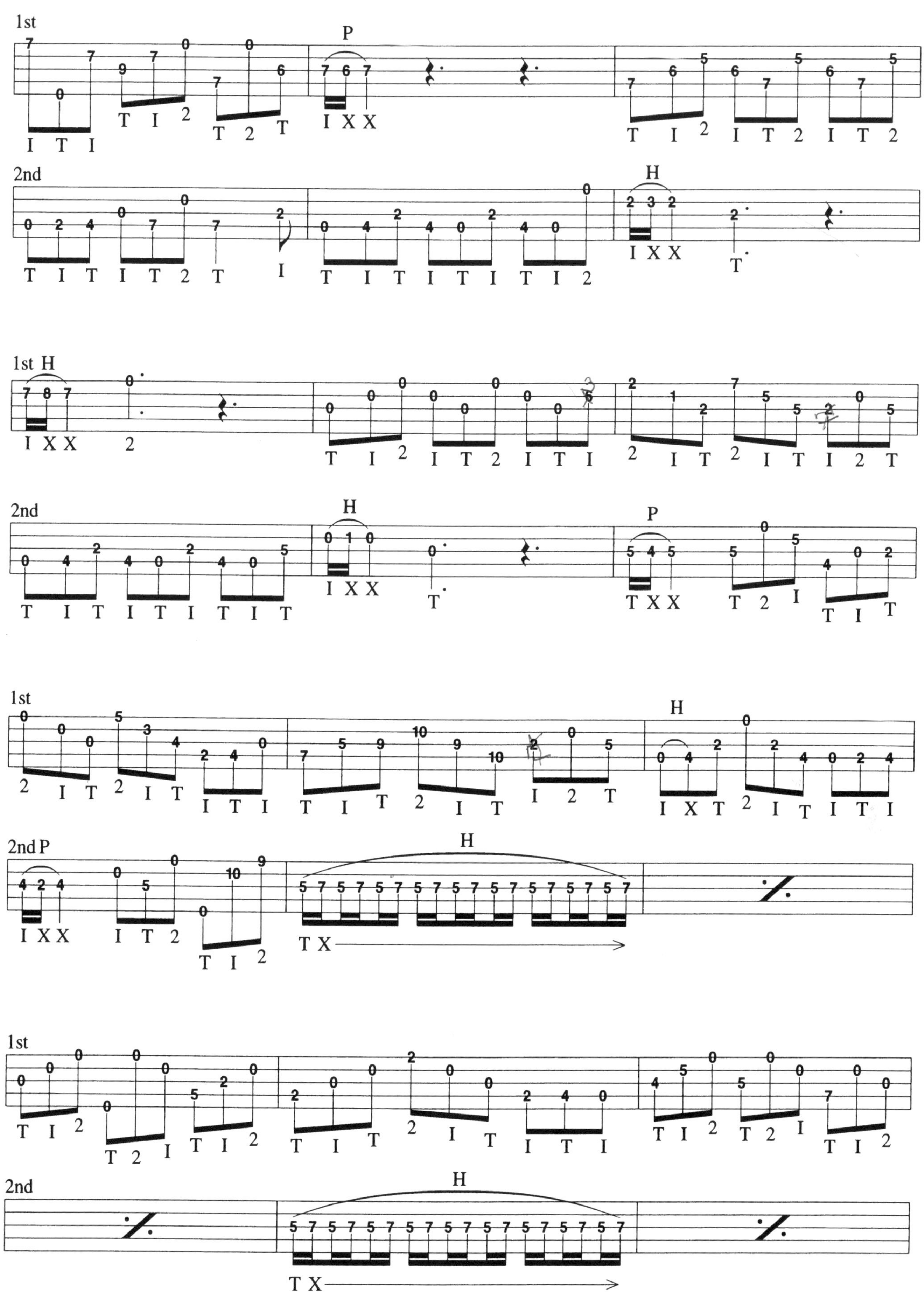
1st
P
2nd
H
1st H
2nd
H
P
1st
H
2nd P
H
1st
2nd
H

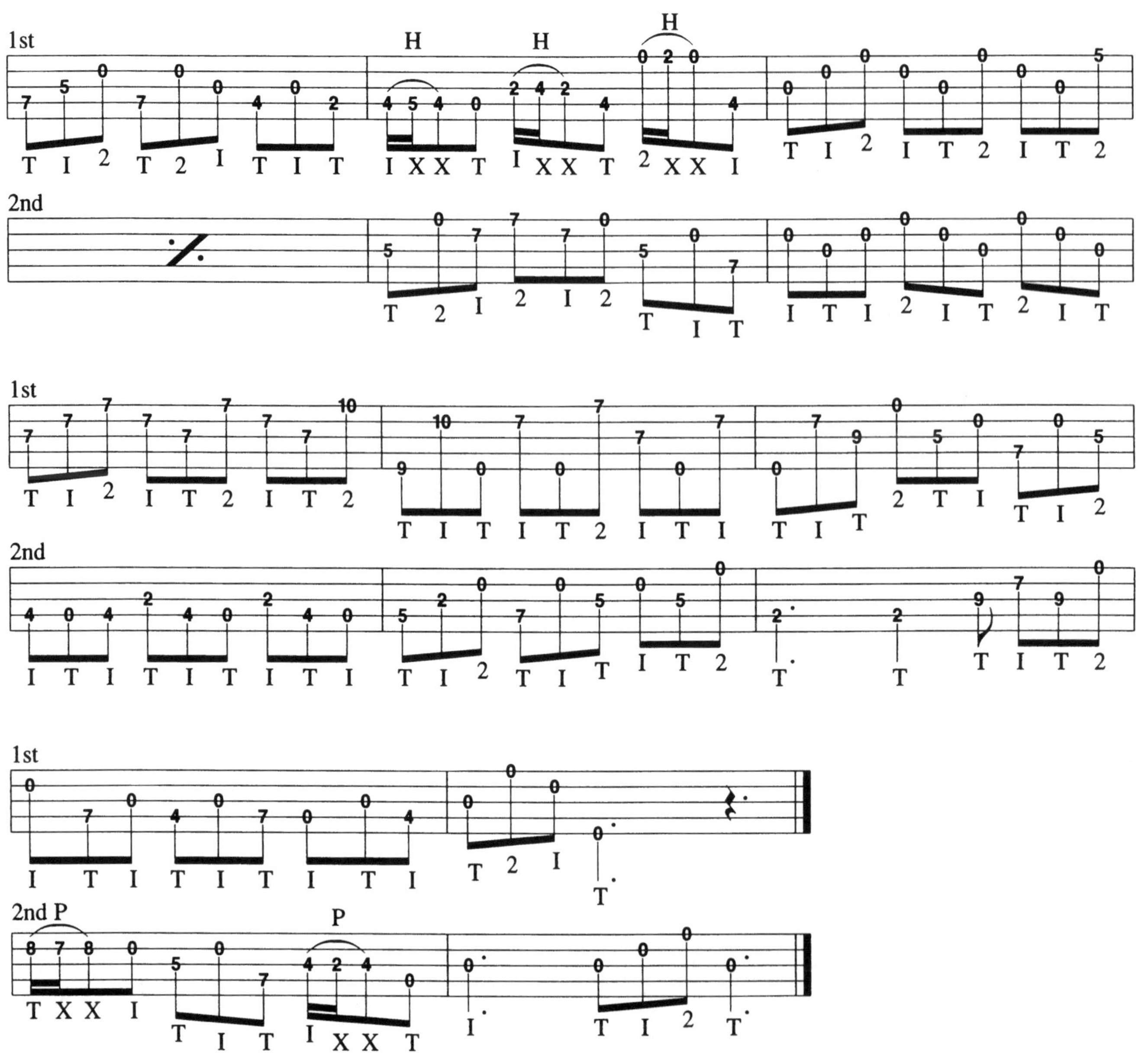
1st
2nd
1st
2nd
1st
2nd

TWO BAROQUE PIECES

Domenico Scarlatti (1685-1757) - Sonata in A minor
Johann Pachelbel (1653-1706) - Canon in D

Although Domenico Scarlatti was an Italian by birth and composed almost exclusively for the harpsichord, he spent more than 40 years in Spain and was deeply influenced by the guitar and by Spanish music in general. These influences can be readily heard in "Sonata in A minor," a short work transcribed for banjo from the classical guitar.

Pachelbel's "Canon in D" is a popular piece which is beautiful in its simplicity and has become a standard in the classical repertoire. This work opens with a basic familiar chord progression that repeats with variations throughout the entire work.

SONATA IN A MINOR

Arranged for banjo
by Larry Vanek
C Tuning

D. Scarlatti

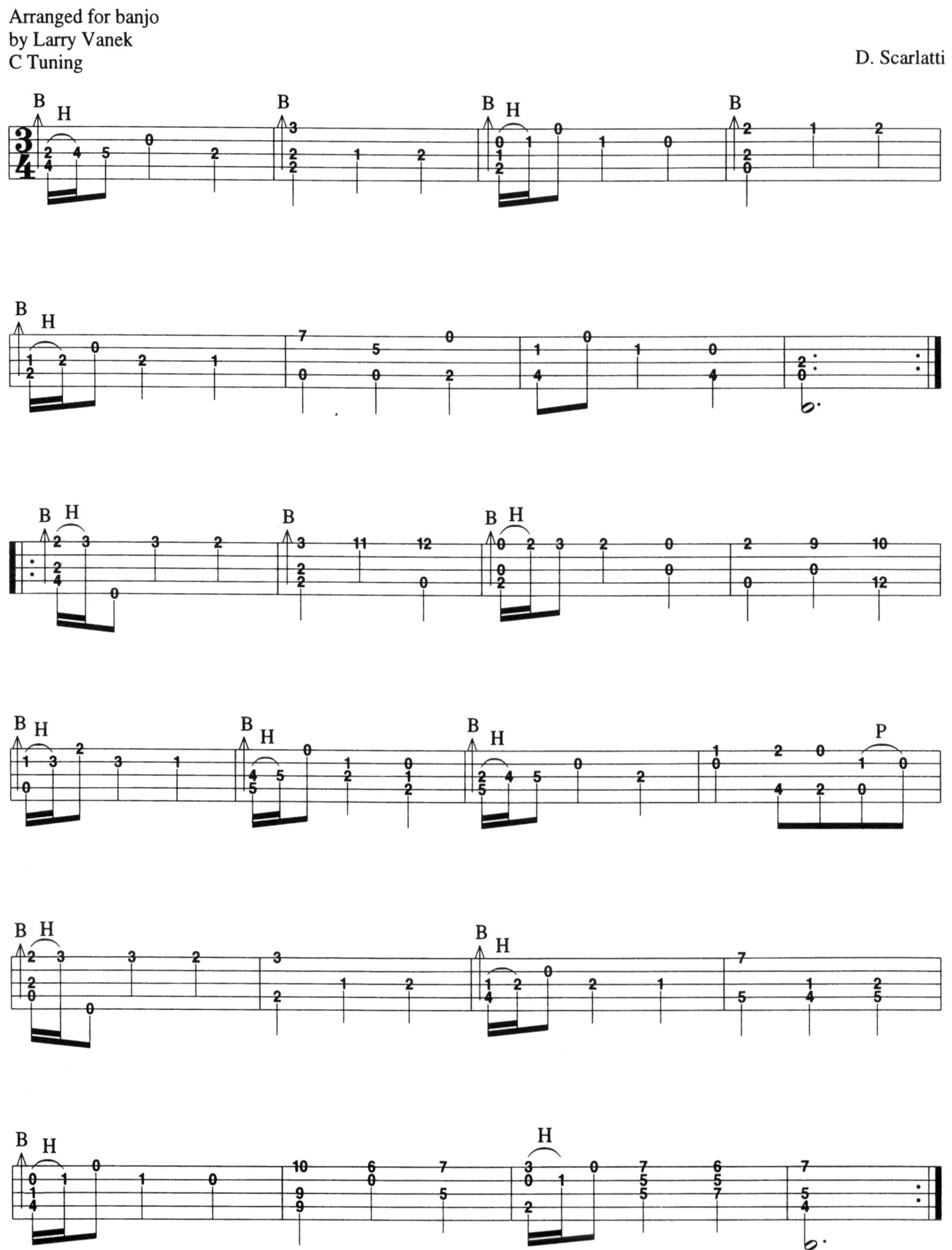

CANON IN D

Arranged for banjo
by Larry Vanek
G Tuning

Johann Pachelbel

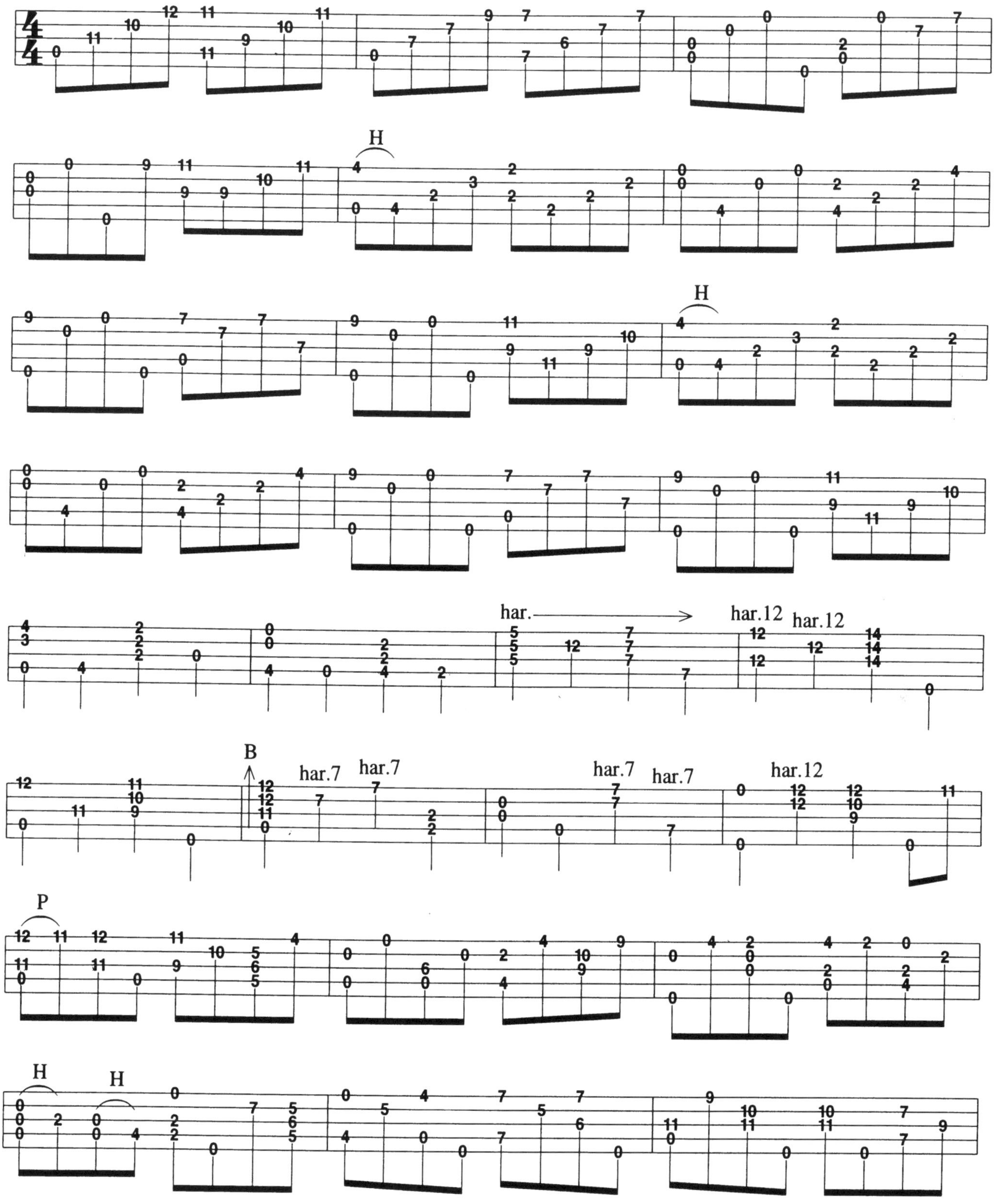

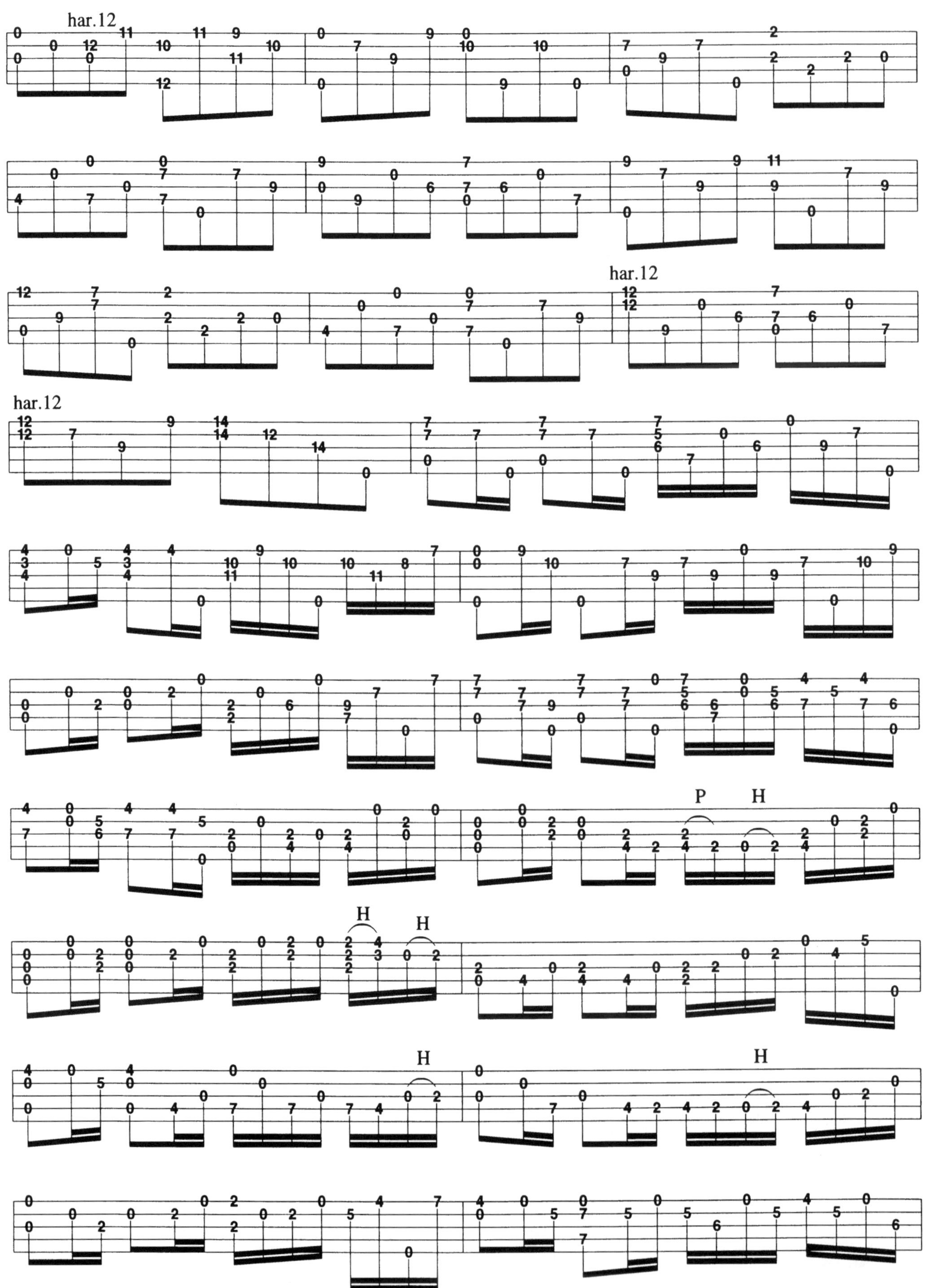
har.12
har.12
har.12
P
H
H
H
H
H

P
P
har.12
har.12
H
P
har.12
har. 17
har.12
B

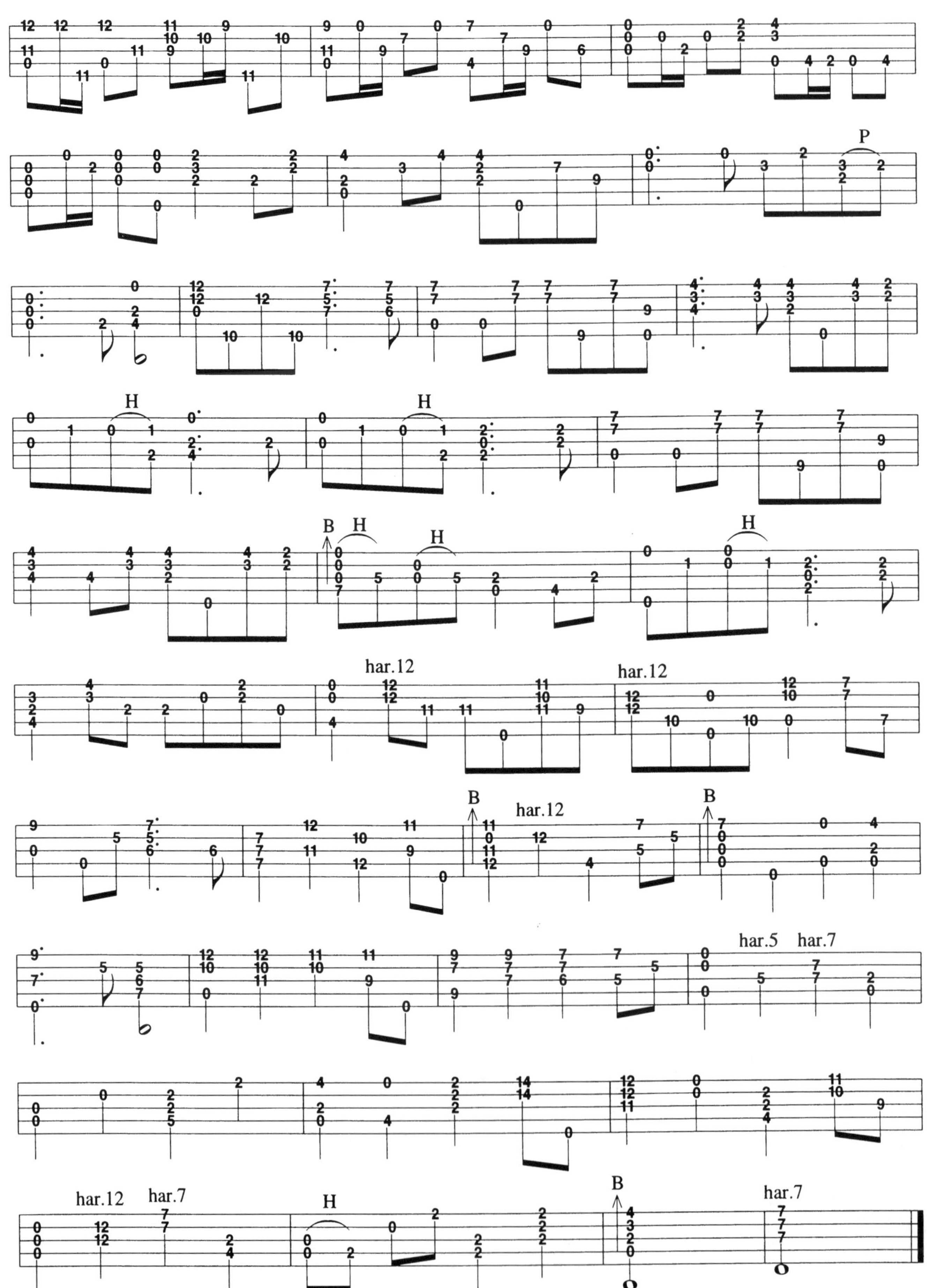
P
H
H
B
H
H
H
har.12
har.12
B
har.12
B
har.5
har.7
har.12
har.7
H
B
har.7

TWO PIECES BY BEETHOVEN (1770-1827)

Fur Elise

Sonata No. 14 (Moonlight Sonata)

These are two well-known pieces by Beethoven that work remarkably well on the five-string banjo. Sonata No. 14, or the "Moonlight Sonata," is one of Beethoven's most familiar works, and the arrangement given here should be well within the grasp of the intermediate player. Eighth note triplets are employed throughout the piece and should be played slowly and with great expression.

FÜR ELISE

Arranged for banjo
by Larry Vanek
C Tuning

Ludwig von Beethoven

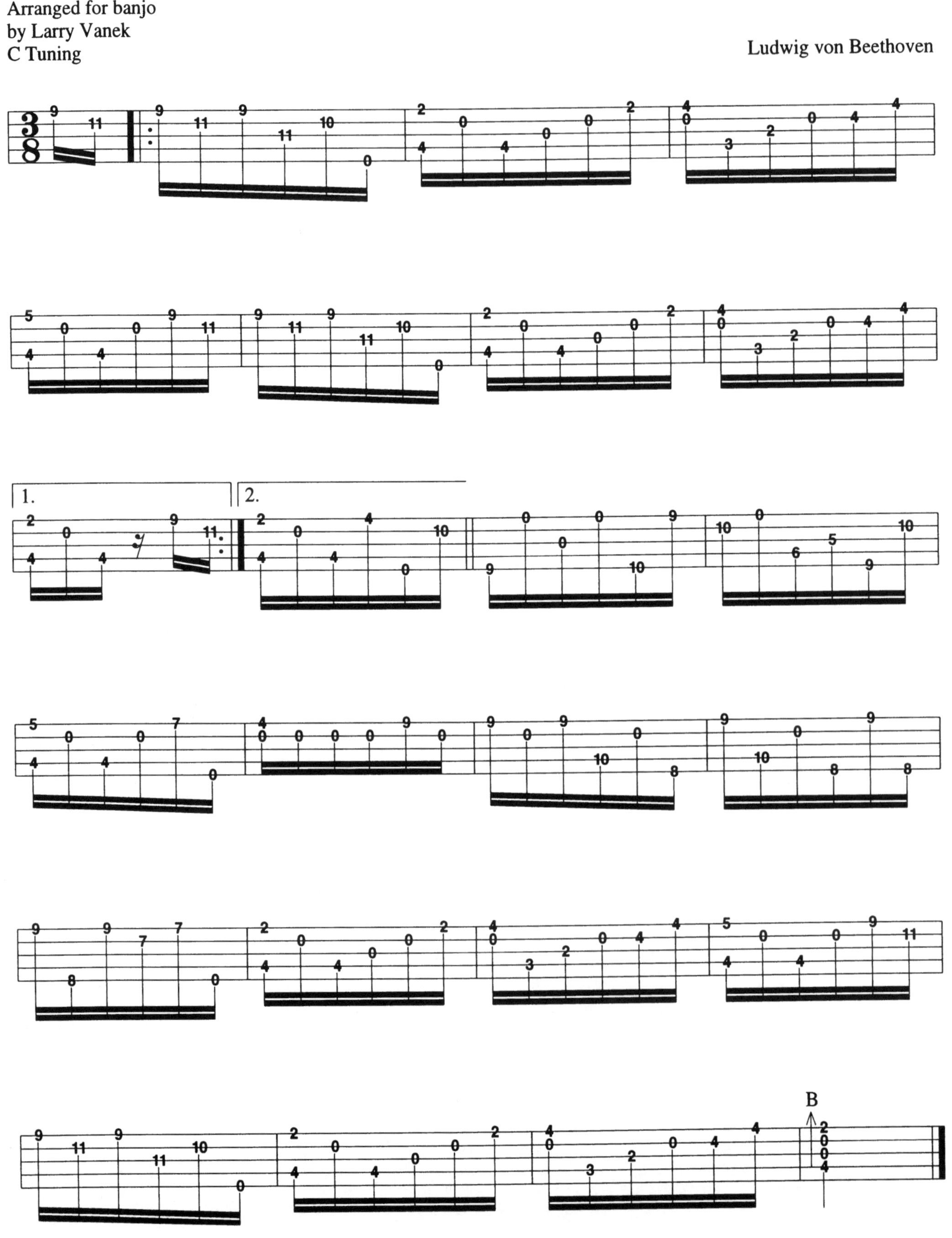

SONATA NO. 14
(Moonlight Sonata)

Arranged for banjo
by Larry Vanek
G Tuning

Ludwig von Beethoven

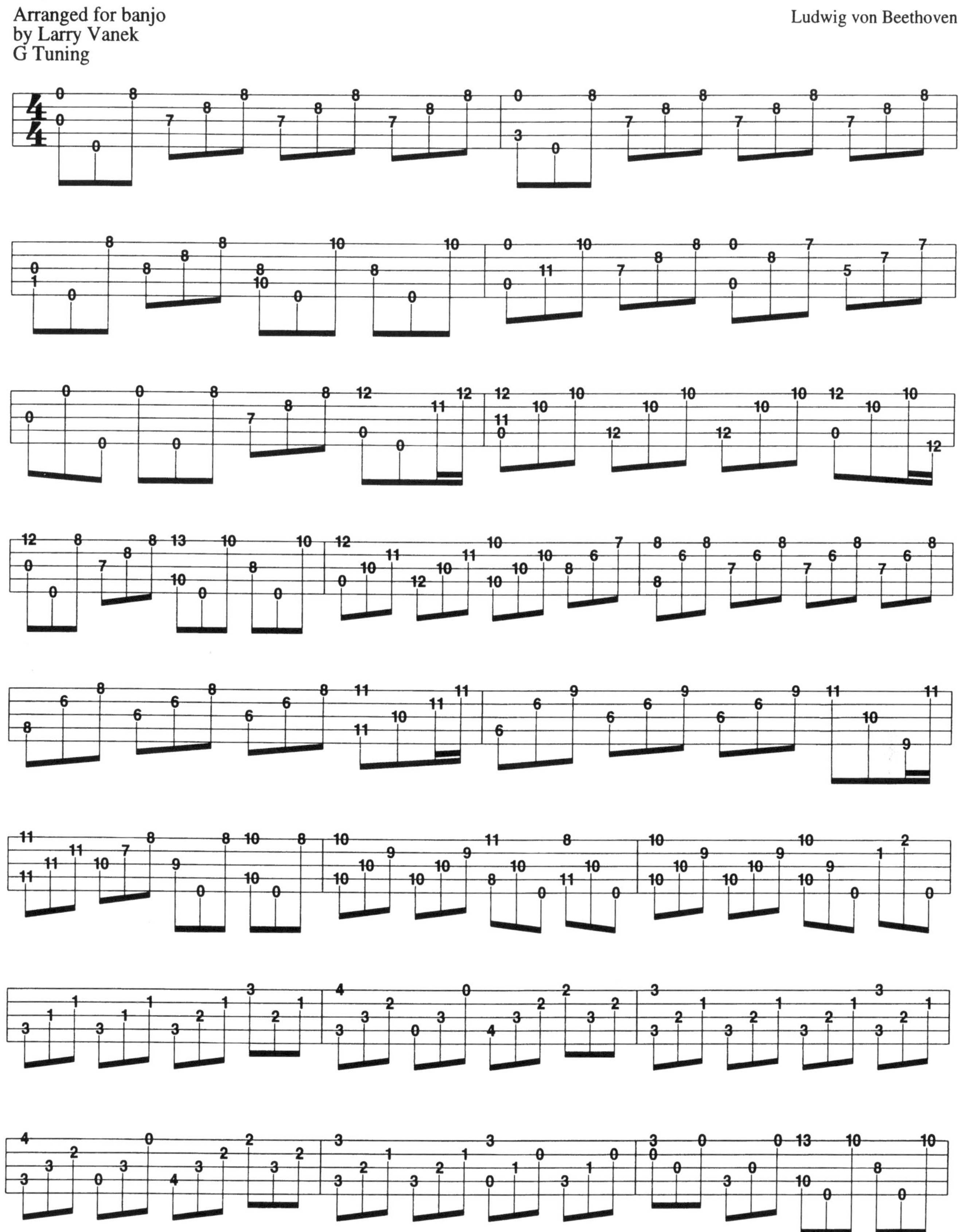

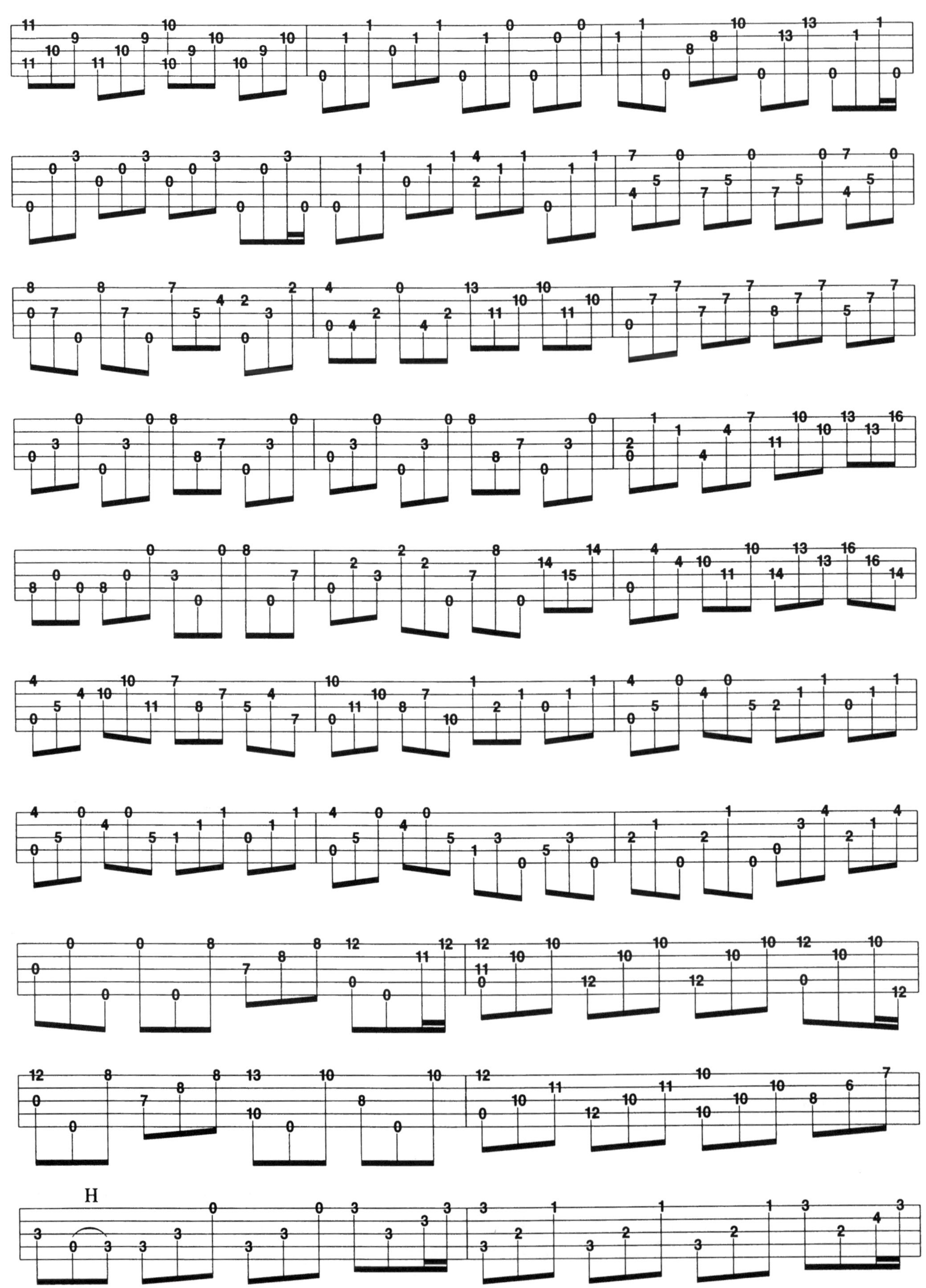
H

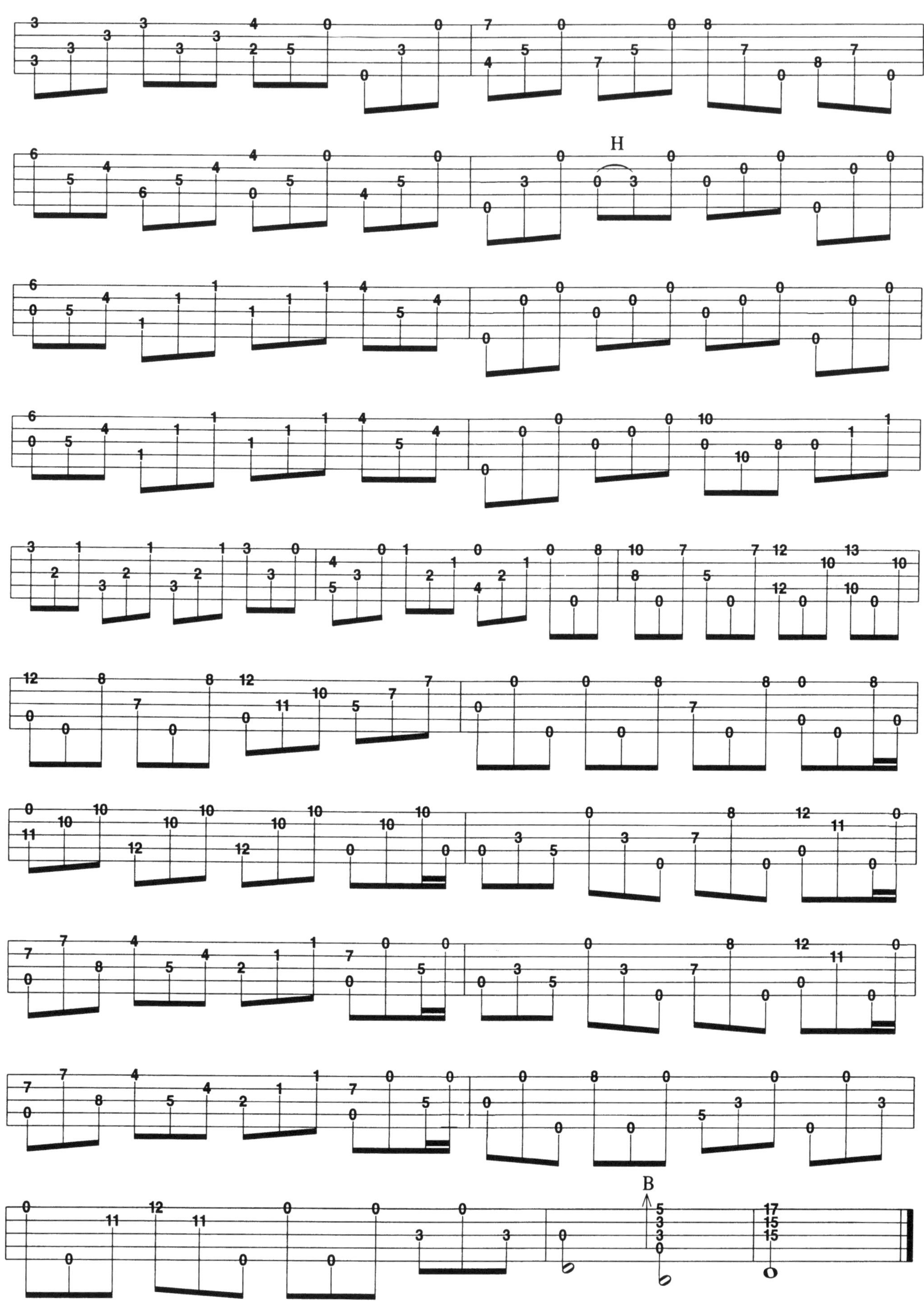

H
B

FOUR WORKS BY RUSSIAN COMPOSERS

Peter Tchaikovsky (1840-1893) - Old French Song, Swan Lake

Mikhail Glinka (1804-1857) - Melody

Modeste Mussorgsky (1839-1881) - An Old Castle

These three Russian composers were roughly contemporaries, with Mikhail Glinka being the initiator of a movement which drew its inspiration from Russian folk music. This movement later came to include a group of composers known as "the Mighty Handful" of which Modeste Mussorgsky was a member, along with Rimsky-Korsakov and Mikhail Borodin. Though Tchaikovsky was a contemporary of these composers, his own work more closely followed traditional European models, although it too contained uniquely Russian characteristics of scale and folk melody. Both the Tchaikovsky and Glinka pieces transcribed here are fairly short and do not pose any difficult technical problems.

Modeste Mussorgsky was an iconoclastic composer whose life ended in poverty, bitterness and complete alcoholic ruin. He is today recognized as the greatest genius of the "Mighty Handful" on the strength of such works as his opera "Boris Godunov" and the piano suite "Pictures at an Exhibition." His music was often marked by sharp dissonances and unusual harmonies and in some cases even imitated the speech patterns of the Russian language. "An Old Castle," from "Pictures at an Exhibition," is the second in a series of musical impressions by Mussorgsky of an exhibition of drawings by the artist Victor Hartmann. Although it was originally written for piano, it is now best known in its orchestrated version by Maurice Ravel. The transcription here was done directly from the piano music, although it has also been transcribed and played on the classical guitar, notably by Andres Segovia and Liona Boyd.

OLD FRENCH SONG

Arranged for banjo
by Larry Vanek
C Tuning

P. Tchaikovsky

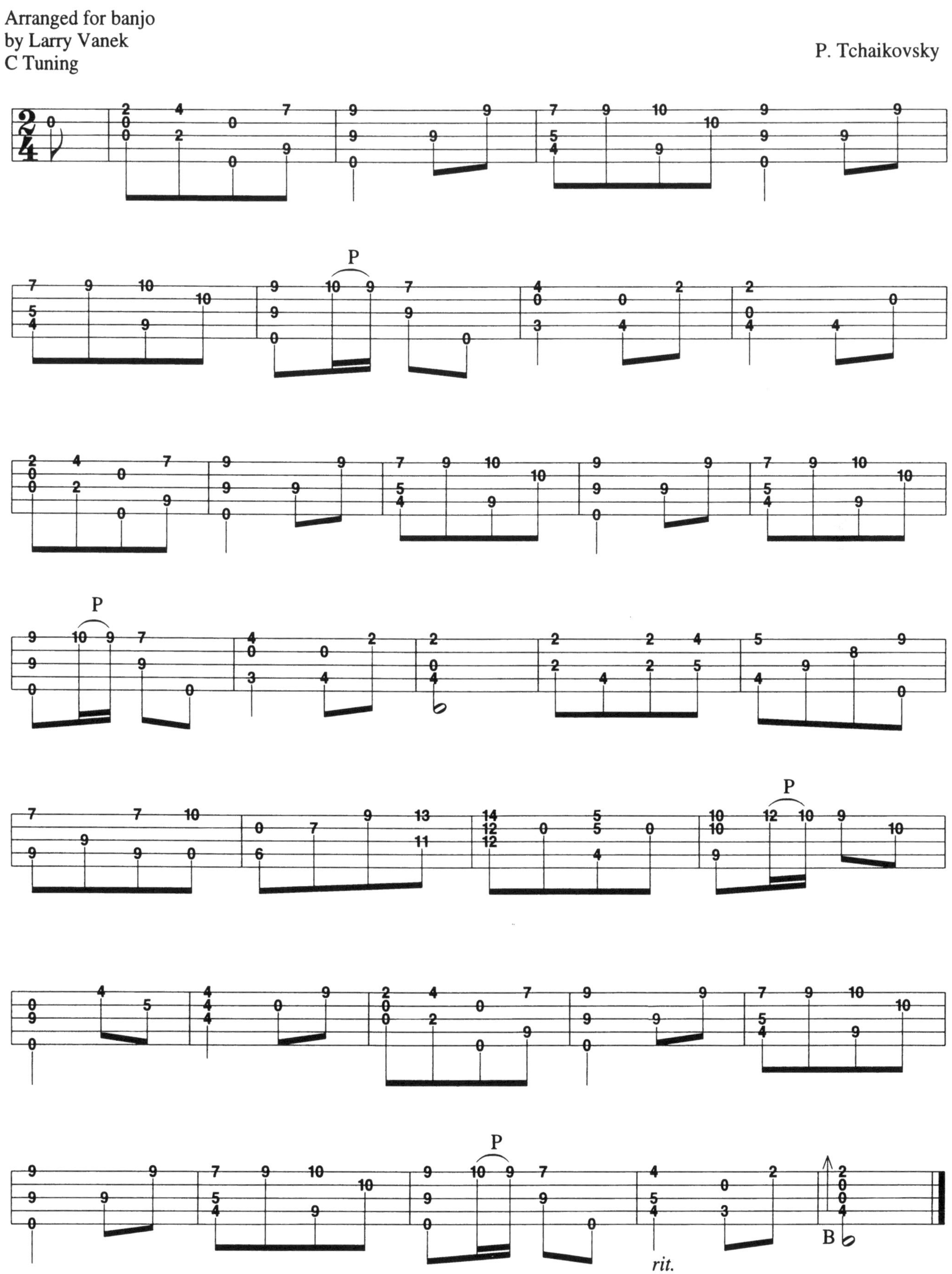

SWAN LAKE

(Theme)

Arranged for banjo
by Larry Vanek
G Tuning

P. Tchaikovsky

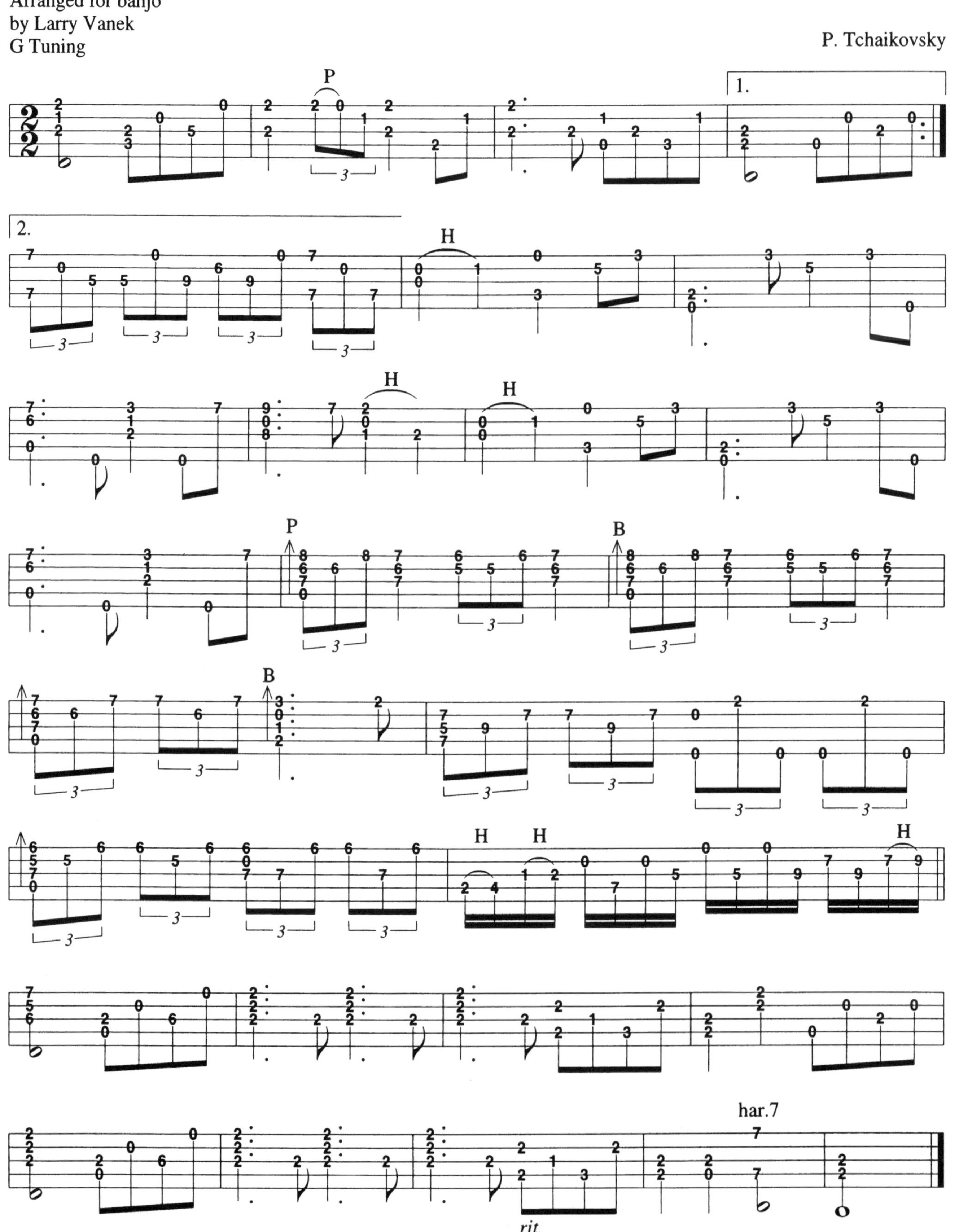

MELODY

Arranged for banjo
by Larry Vanek
C Tuning

M. Glinka

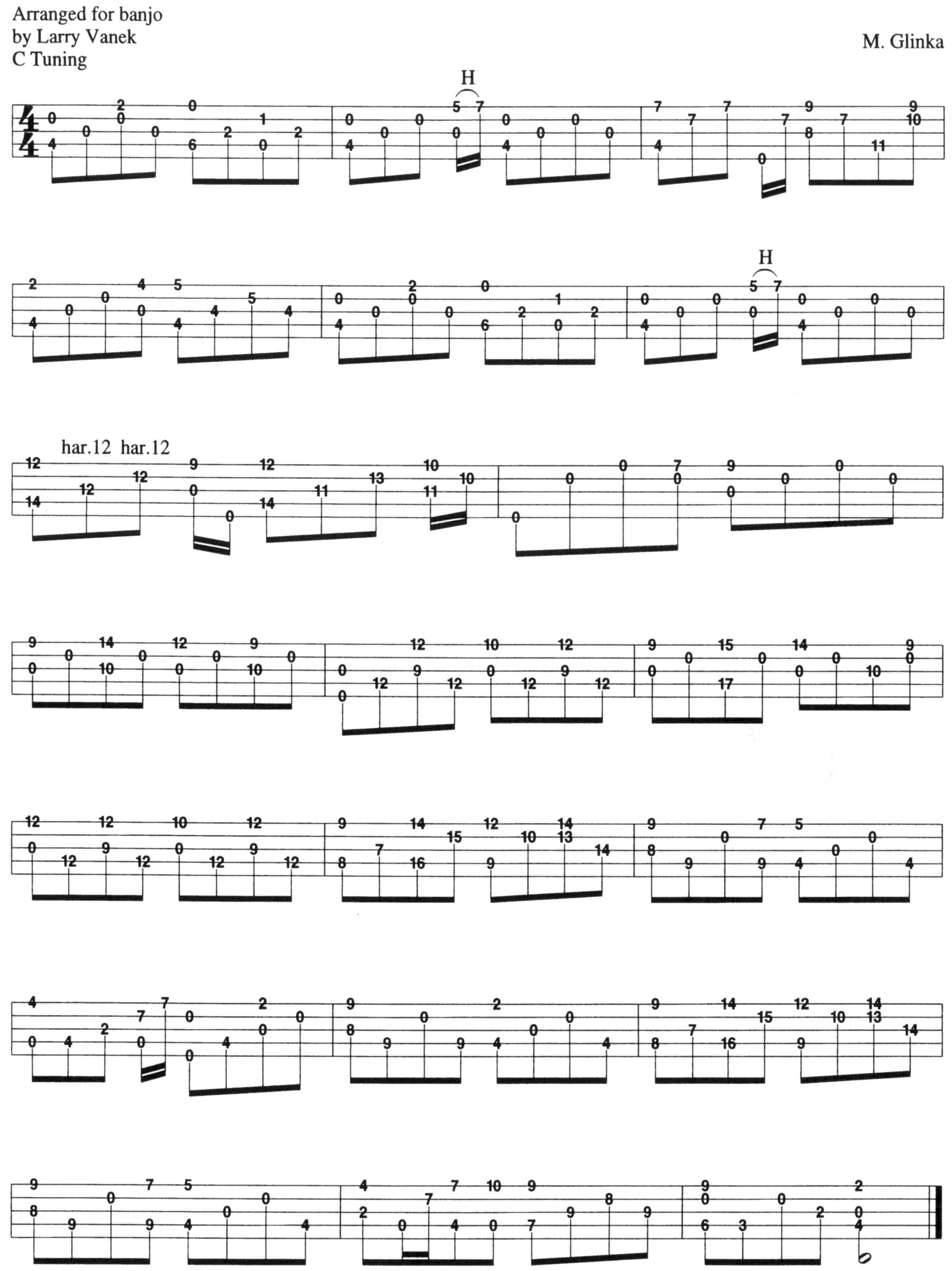

AN OLD CASTLE

(from Pictures at an Exhibition)

Arranged for banjo
by Larry Vanek
C Tuning

M. Mussorgsky

B
P
H
G
T I T

rit.
har.5

FIVE WORKS FROM SPAIN

Four works by Spanish Composer Francisco Tarrega (1854-1916)

Adelita, Lagrima, Capricho Arabe, and Maria

Enrique Granados (1867-1916) - Spanish Dance No. 2 (Oriental)

These four pieces by the Spanish guitarist and composer Francisco Tarrega occupy an exalted place in the classical guitar repertoire. Tarrega himself is considered by many to have been one of the three greatest masters of the classical guitar of all time, the other two being Fernando Sor and Andres Segovia.

All four works are exceptionally beautiful, and of the four "Adelita" and "Lagrima" are the easiest, with both "Capricho Arabe" and "Maria" being considerably more difficult. "Maria" especially demands some difficult left hand stretches due to the tuning employed (fourth string tuned down to B) and also utilizes the entire range of the banjo. However, in view of the innate beauty of this piece, I think you will find the technical demands well worth the trouble.

"Capricho Arabe" is fairly lengthy but somewhat less difficult than "Maria." It employs elements of both melodic and single string style and uses quite a few musical symbols which may not be readily familiar, so you may need to refer to the section on notation and terminology which appears at the beginning of this book. For the intermediate player, this piece may also be considerably shortened by playing the first section to the second repeat sign as a complete solo in itself.

Enrique Granados was a member of "the Big Three," composers of a Spanish nationalist school, who died tragically on a torpedoed English ocean liner while on the way to America to perform for President Woodrow Wilson. "Spanish Dance No. 2" was originally written for piano and exhibits many of the characteristics of Spanish music. I think it adapts especially well to the five-string banjo due to the strong influence of the guitar in much Spanish music. The "D.C." sign which appears at the end of the piece means to repeat the 3/4 section from the beginning.

A fine recording of this work for two guitars exists on "Music for the Classical Guitar" by Ida Presti and Alexandre Lagoya on Nonesuch Records.

ADELITA

Arranged for banjo
by Larry Vanek
G Tuning

F. Tarrega

LAGRIMA

Arranged for banjo
by Larry Vanek
G Tuning
4th string down to B

F. Tarrega

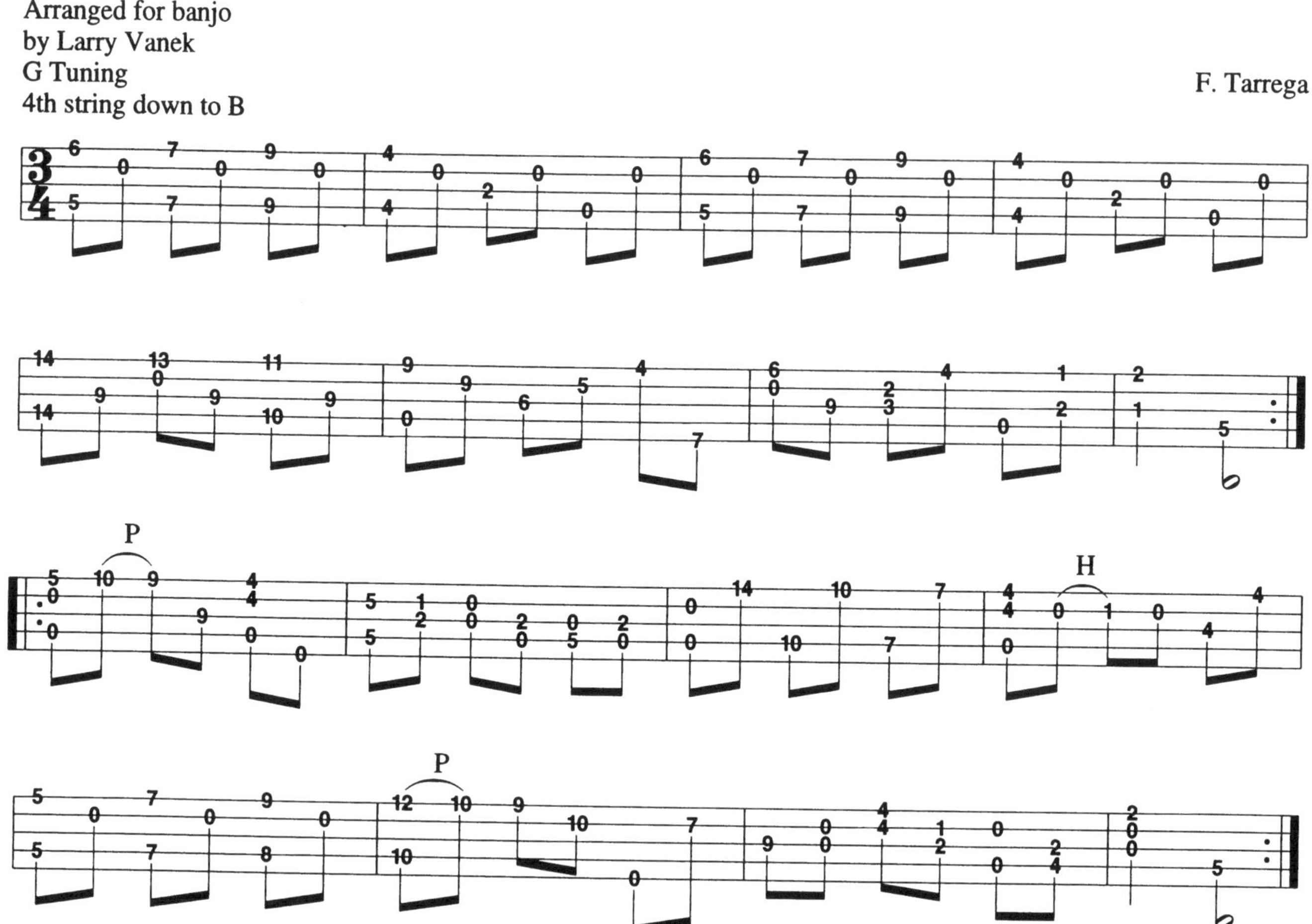

CAPRICHO ARABE

Arranged for banjo
by Larry Vanek
C Tuning

F. Tarrega

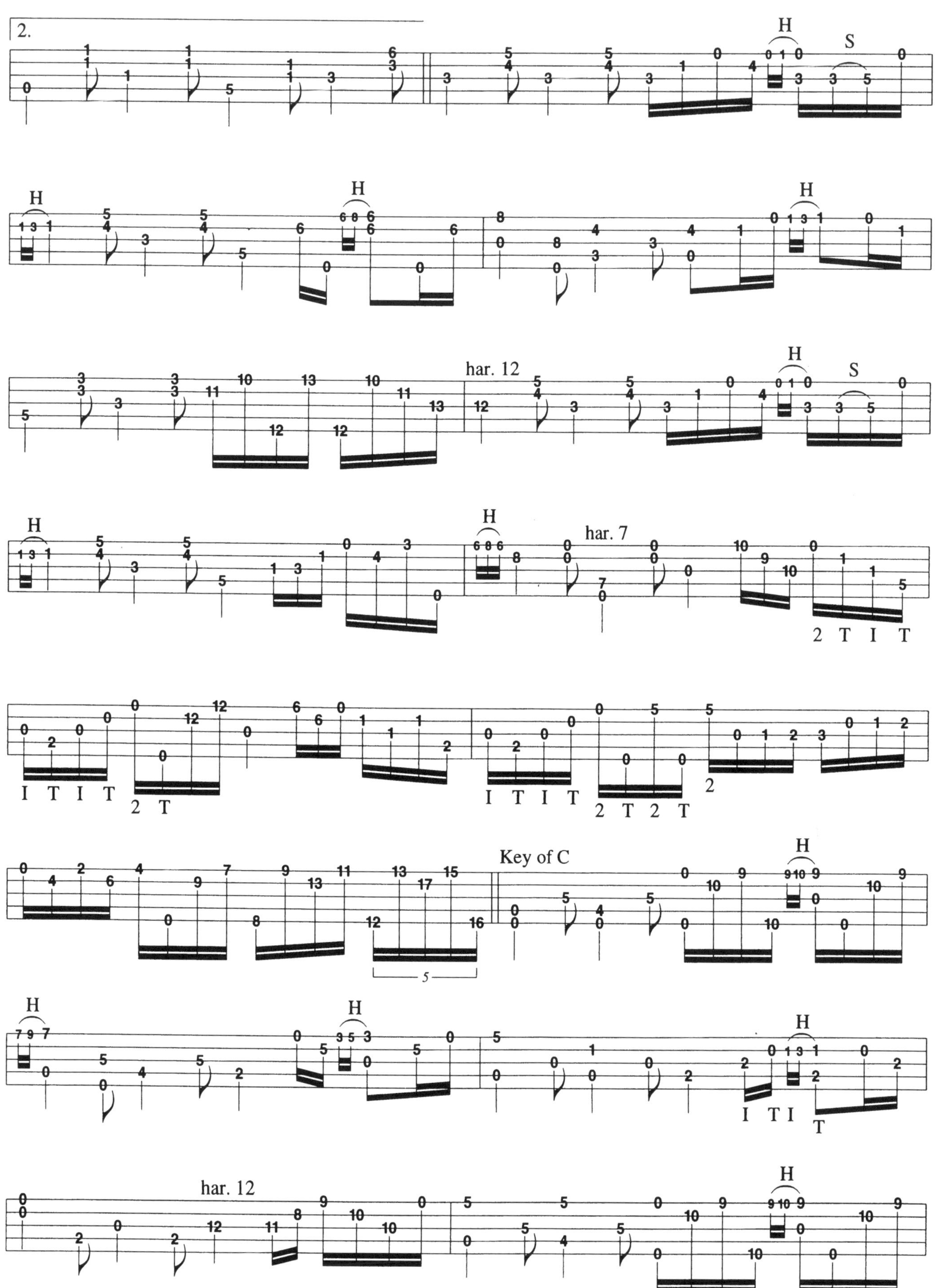
2.
H
S
H
H
H
har. 12
H
S
H
H
har. 7
2 T I T
I T I T
2 T
I T I T
2 T 2 T
2
Key of C
H
5
H
H
H
I T I
T
har. 12
H

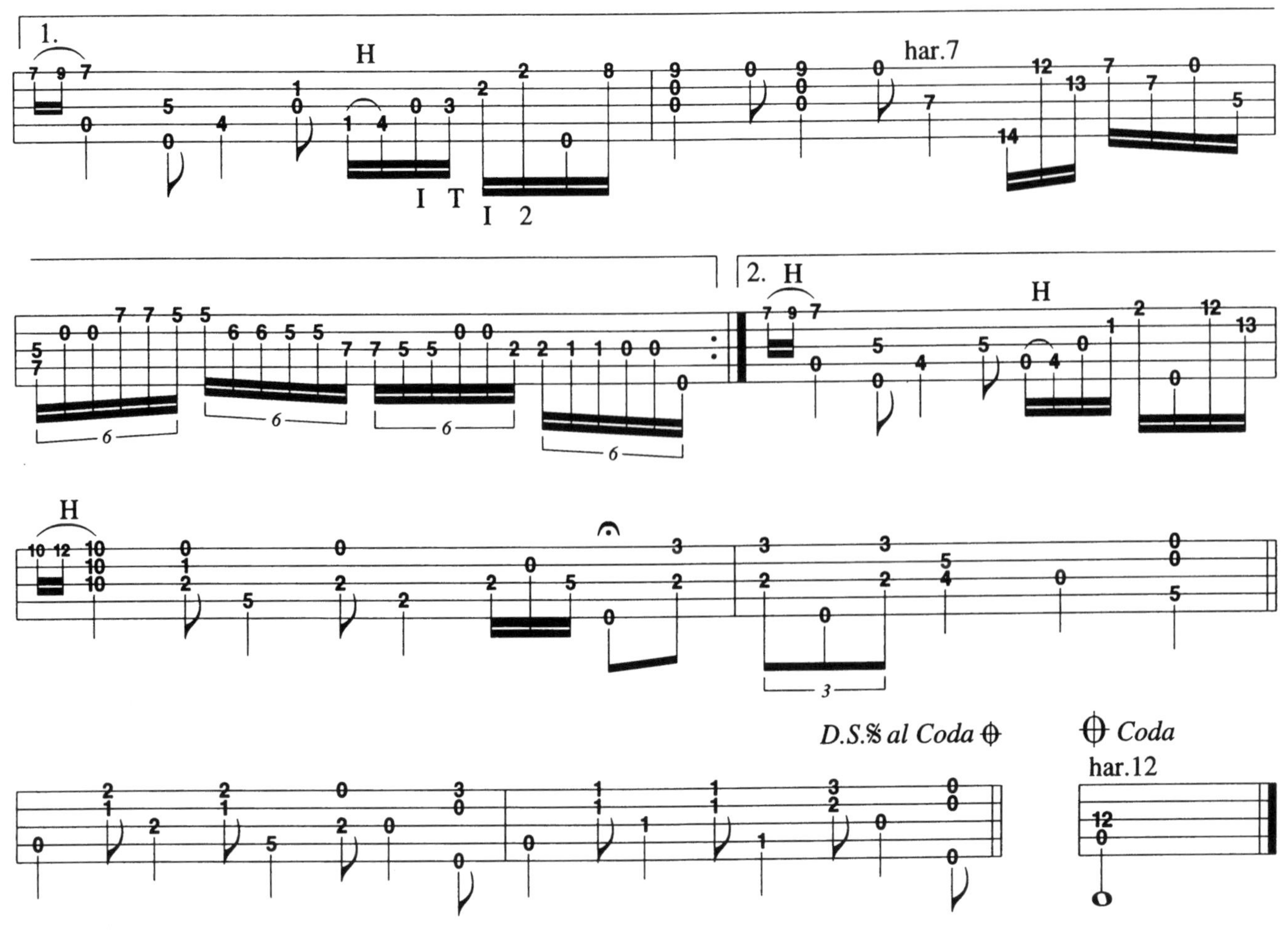
1.
H
har.7
I T
I 2
2. H
H
H
D.S.𝄋 al Coda
Coda
har.12

This page has been left blank to avoid awkward page turns

MARIA

Arranged for banjo
by Larry Vanek
G Tuning
4th string down to B

F. Tarrega

har.7
P
S
H
G
H
har.12
har.12
B
T I T I

SPANISH DANCE NO. 2

(Oriental)

Arranged for banjo
by Larry Vanek
C Tuning

E. Granados

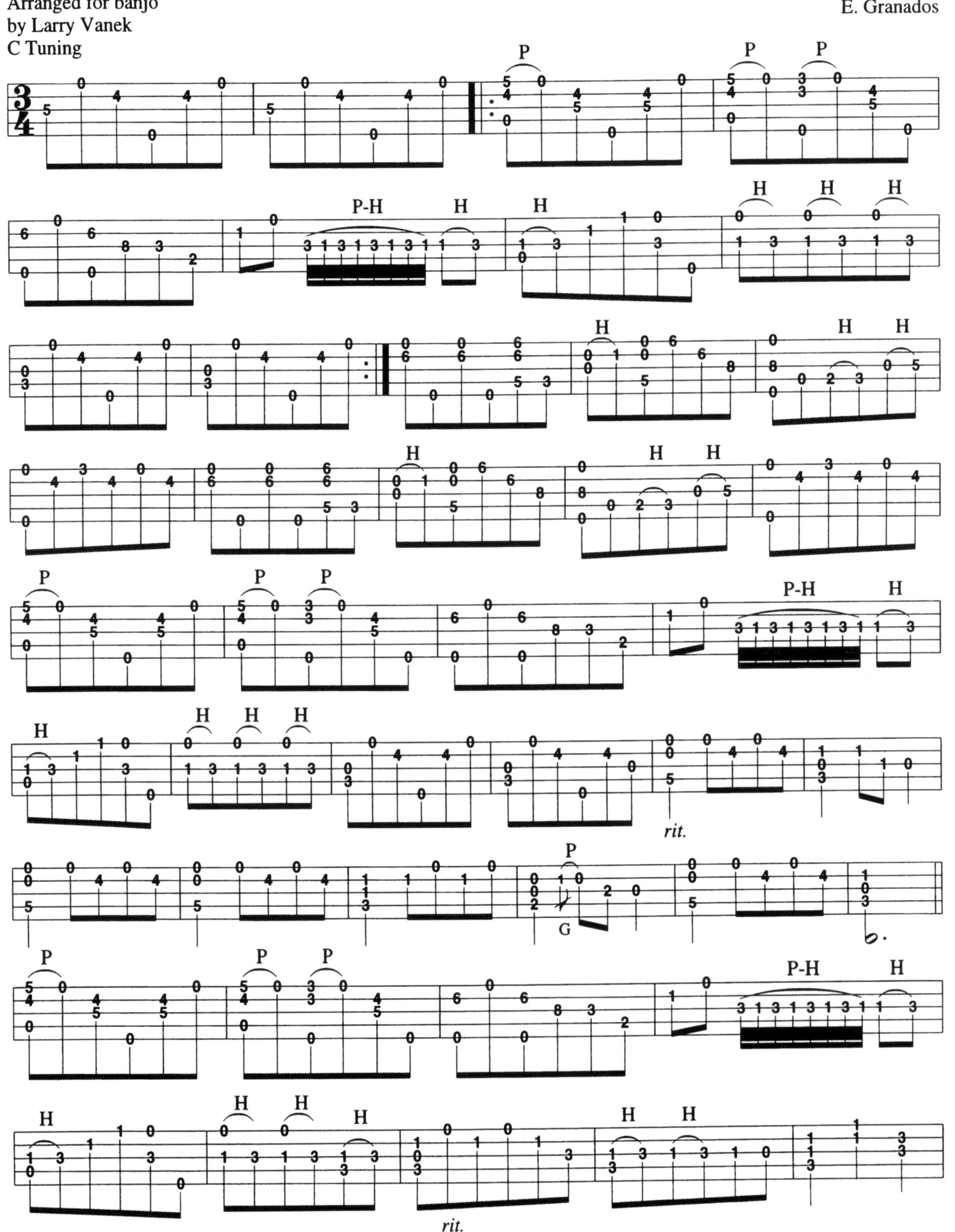

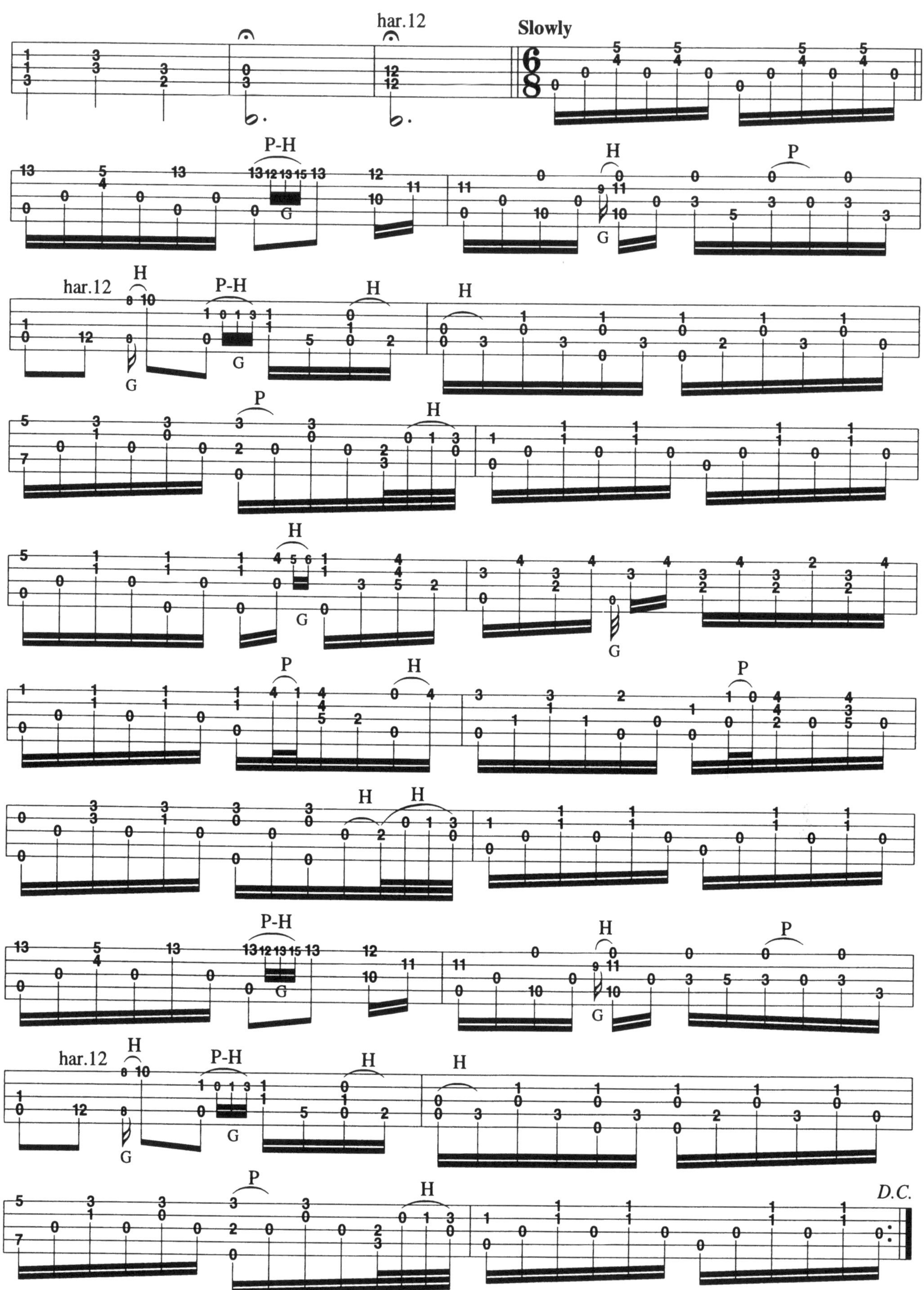

har.12
Slowly
P-H
H
P
G
D.C.

FOUR WORKS BY FRENCH IMPRESSIONISTS

Claude Debussy (1862-1918) - Reverie, Clair de Lune (Moonlight)

Maurice Ravel (1875-1937) - Pavane for a Dead Princess

Gabriel Faure (1845-1924) - Sicilienne (from Pelleas et Melisande)

The French impressionist group of composers roughly paralleled other nationalistic movements in music in Russia, Spain and elsewhere, all being a reaction to the dominance of such German composers as Johannes Brahms and Richard Wagner. Their music was characterized by the innovative use of new scales such as the whole tone scale, the use of parallel fourths and fifths, and the use of extended chords and unconventional chord progressions which later were to influence many modern jazz musicians such as saxophonist John Coltrane.

Claude Debussy was the leader of this school of music and its most famous exponent. The two works transcribed here were originally written for piano but are probably more well known in their orchestral versions by Debussy's friend and contemporary, Maurice Ravel. Both exhibit the vague, dreamlike quality common to much of Debussy's music and impressionist music in general. Rhythmically, the emotional content of these two pieces should take precedence over a strict sense of timing. A less difficult but still esthetically satisfying version of "Reverie" may be played by leaving out the section from L6-M2, p.42, to L3-M2, p.43. For those who enjoy a challenge and wish to play the piece in its entirety, I have left these measures intact in this arrangement despite their relative difficulty. As a final note, since your banjo probably does not include a 24th fret, the harmonic at the end of "Reverie" can easily be found by mentally extending the length of the fingerboard to the 24th fret. This note can also be found as a harmonic on the first string, fifth fret.

Ravel's "Pavane for a Dead Princess" was written for solo piano but later gained more popularity in orchestral form. A pavane is defined as a slow dance of 16th century Spanish origin in 2/4 time, so it should be kept in mind that this piece should be played at a slow tempo. This is a fairly complex piece which contains many interesting chords composed of four notes, so I have made extensive use of the brush technique. As another option, the player could forego the use of fingerpicks and pluck these chords with four fingers, a technique that may well lend itself more advantageously to the soft, dreamlike quality common to much impressionist music.

Gabriel Faure was another member of the circle of friends and composers which included Ravel and Debussy. "Sicilienne" possesses both a harmonic originality and beauty of melodic line that is characteristic of Faure's work.

REVERIE

Arranged for banjo
by Larry Vanek
G Tuning

C. Debussy

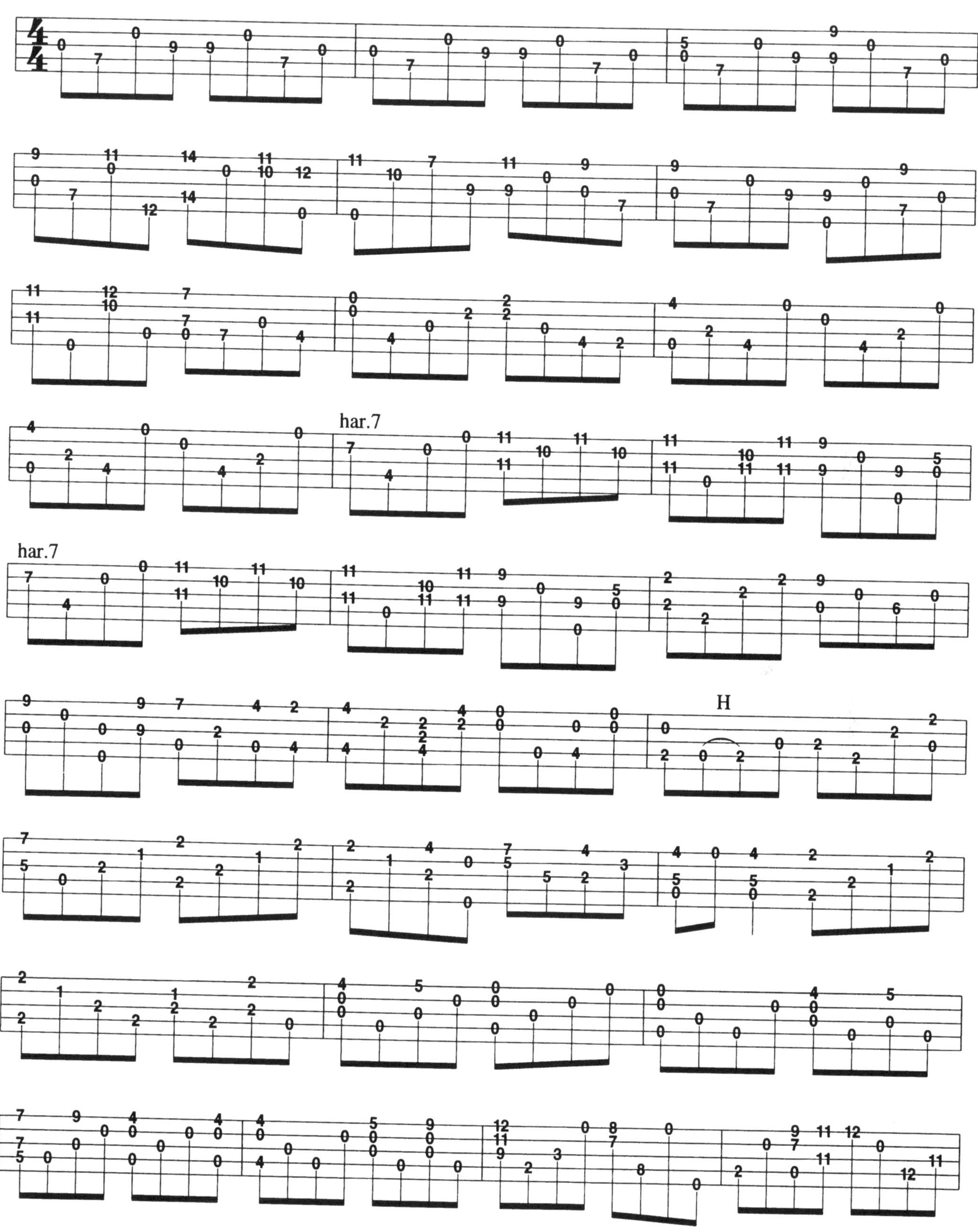

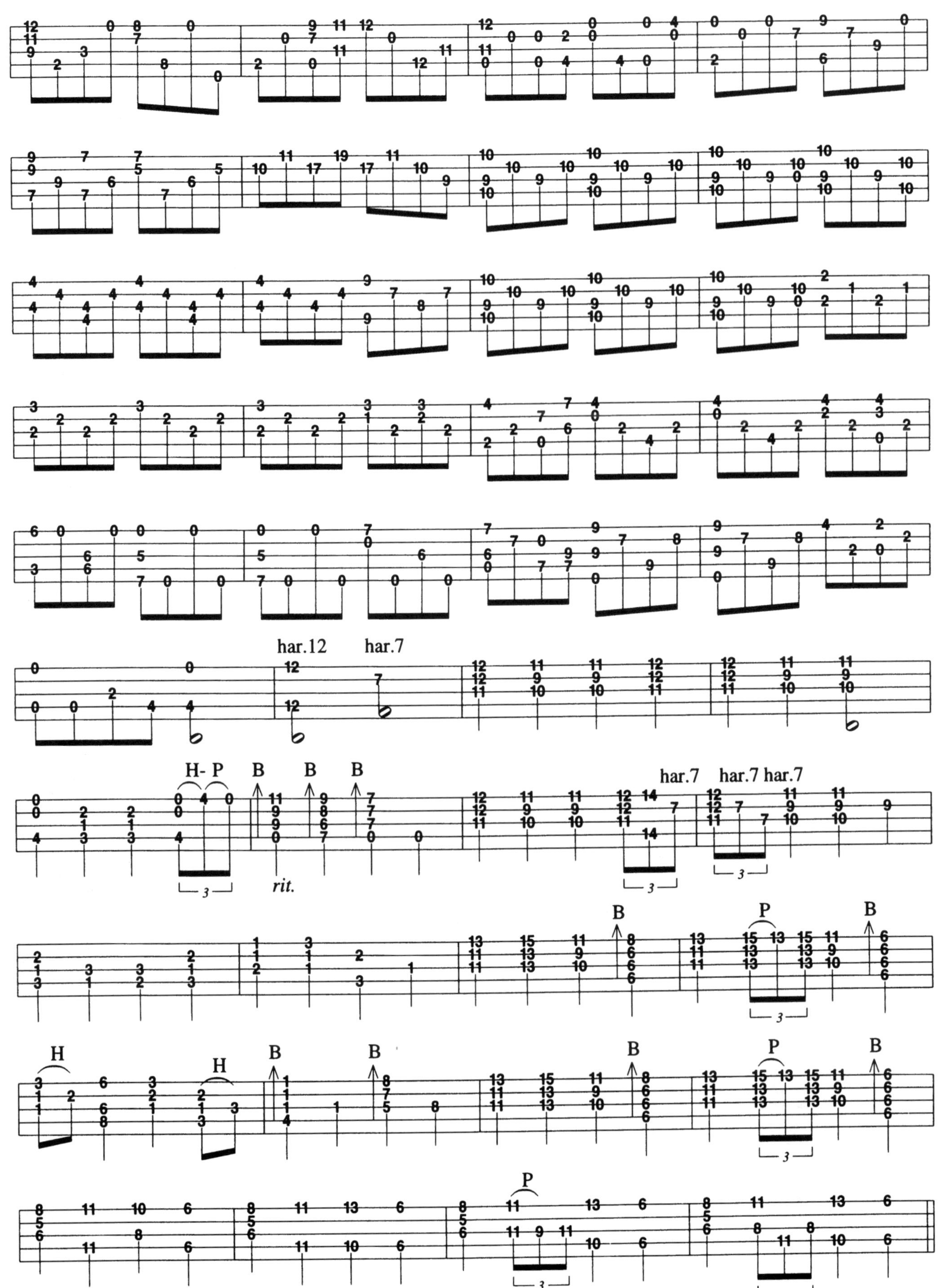

har.12
har.7
H- P
B
rit.
har.7
har.7 har.7
P
H

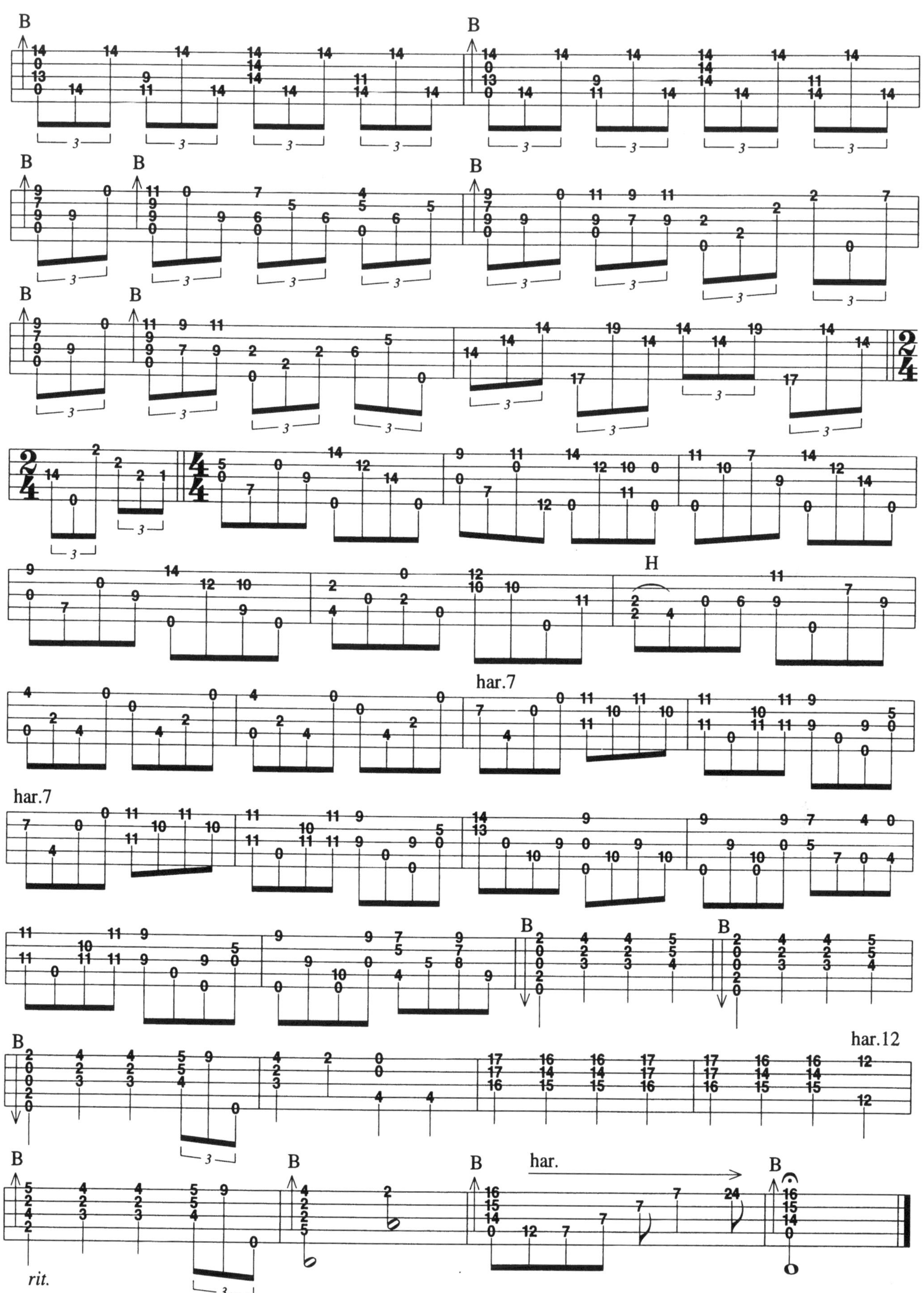

har.7
har.12
har.
rit.

CLAIR DE LUNE
(Moonlight)

Arranged for banjo
by Larry Vanek
G Tuning

C. Debussy

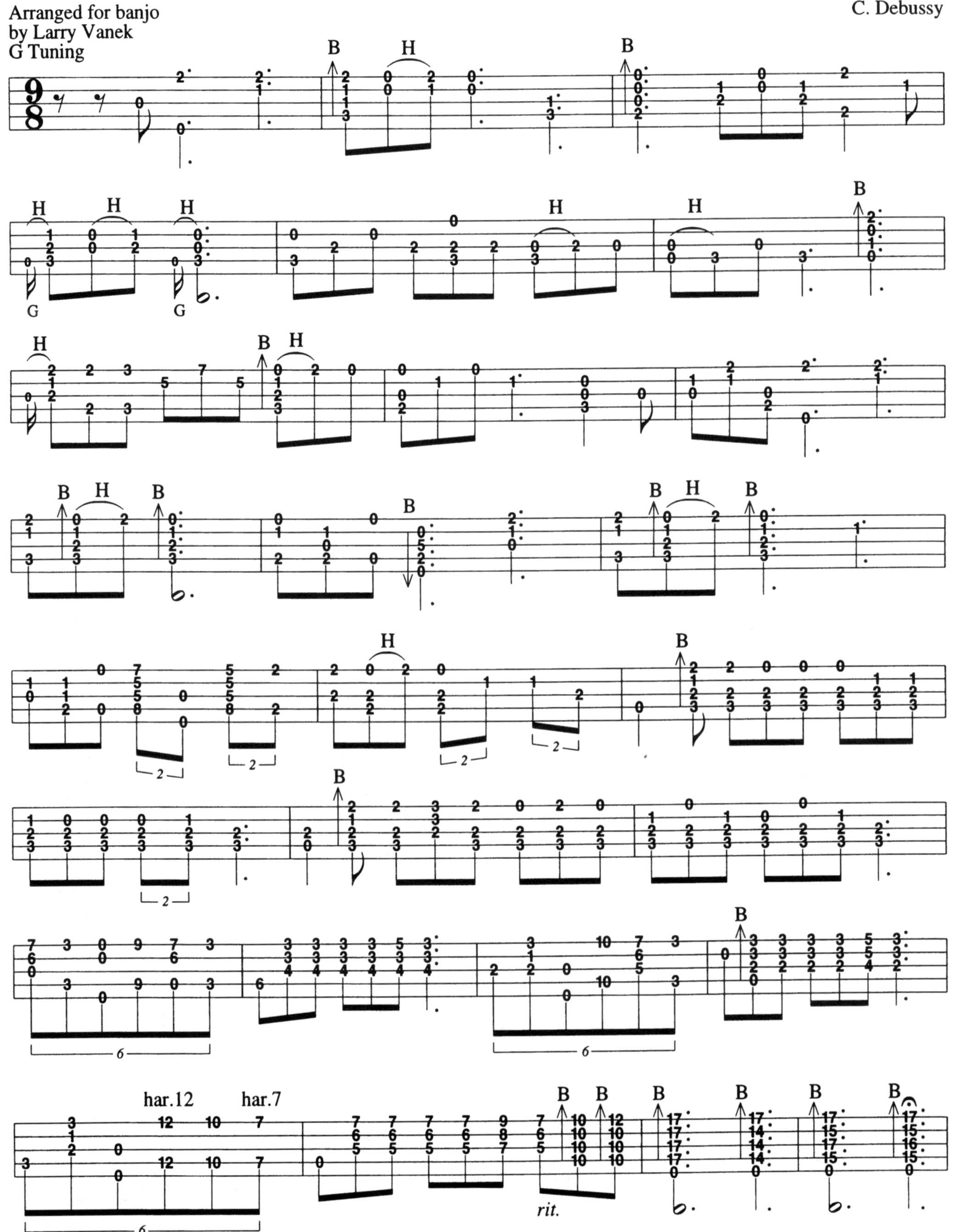

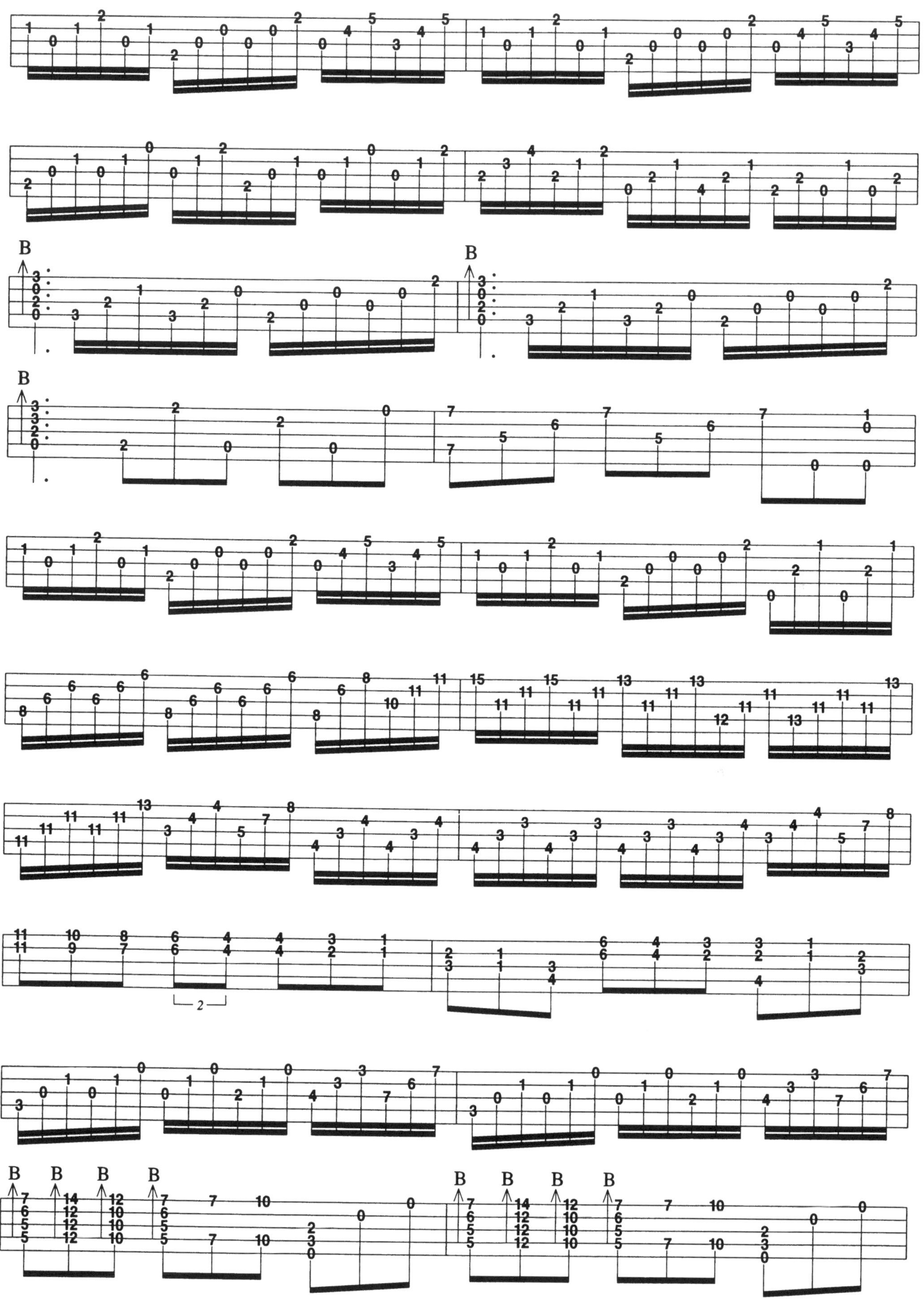
B
B
B
B
B
B
B
B
B
B
B

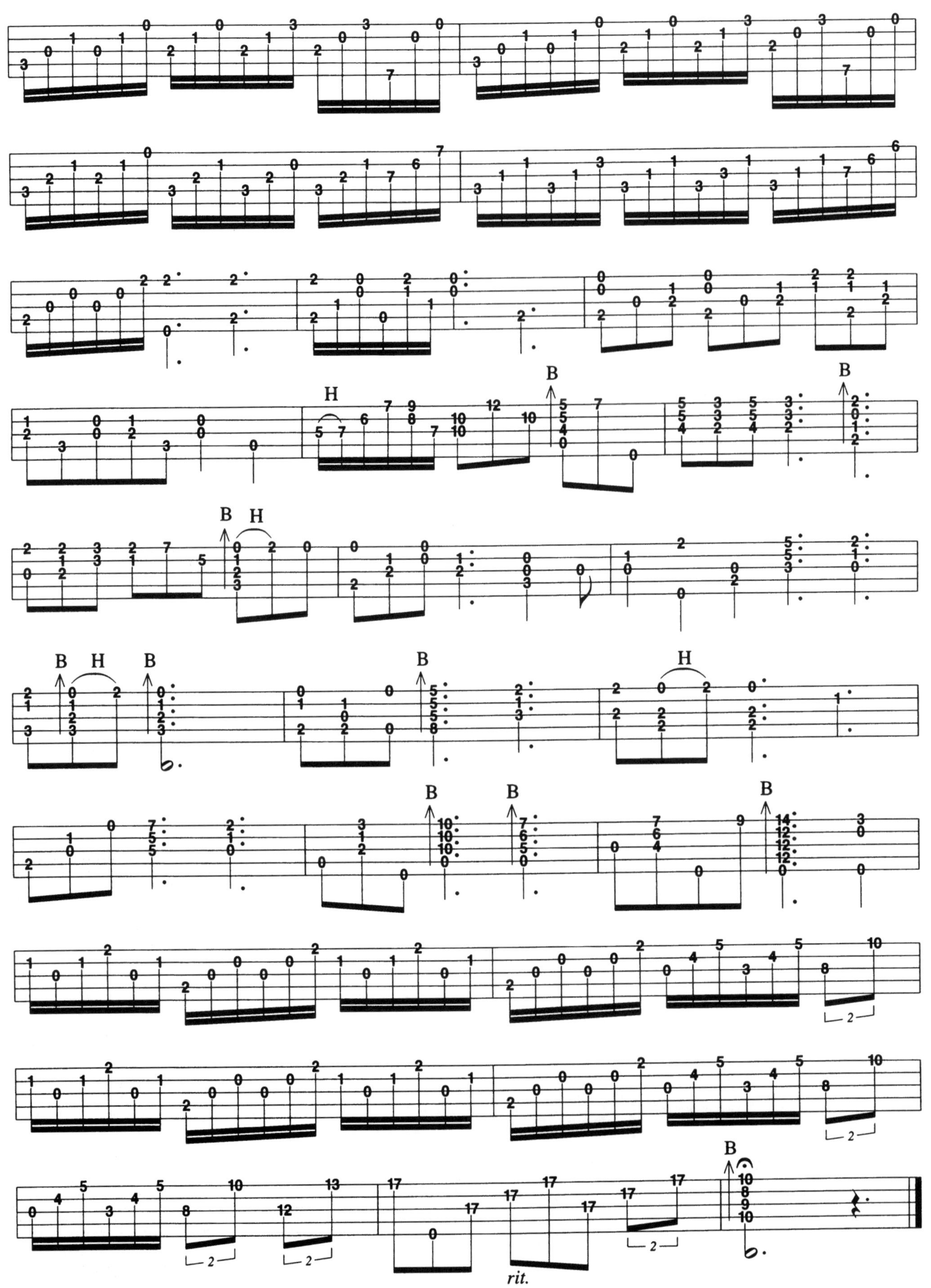
H
B
B
B
H
B
H
B
B
H
B
B
B
rit.
B

PAVANE FOR A DEAD PRINCESS

Arranged for banjo
by Larry Vanek
G Tuning

M. Ravel

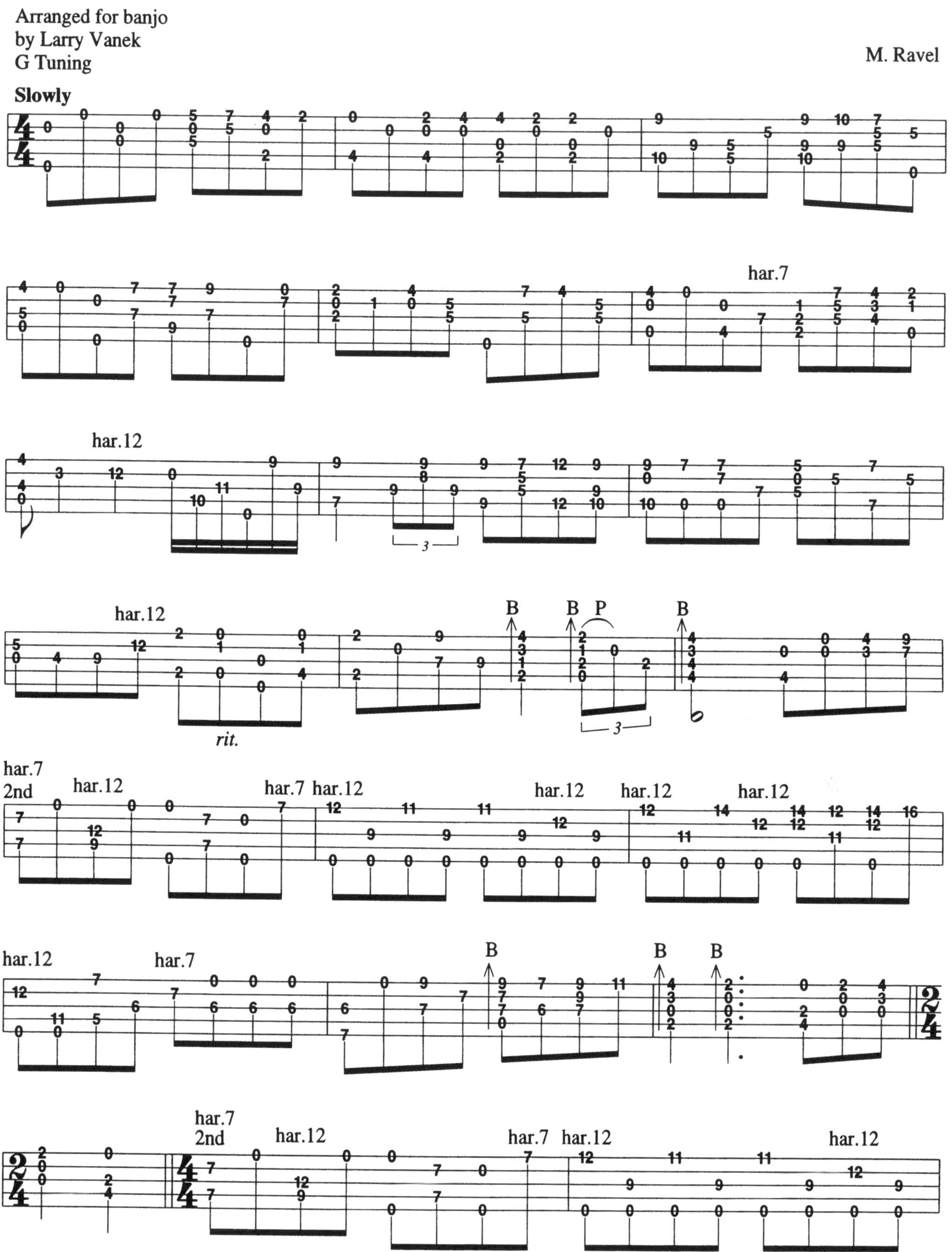

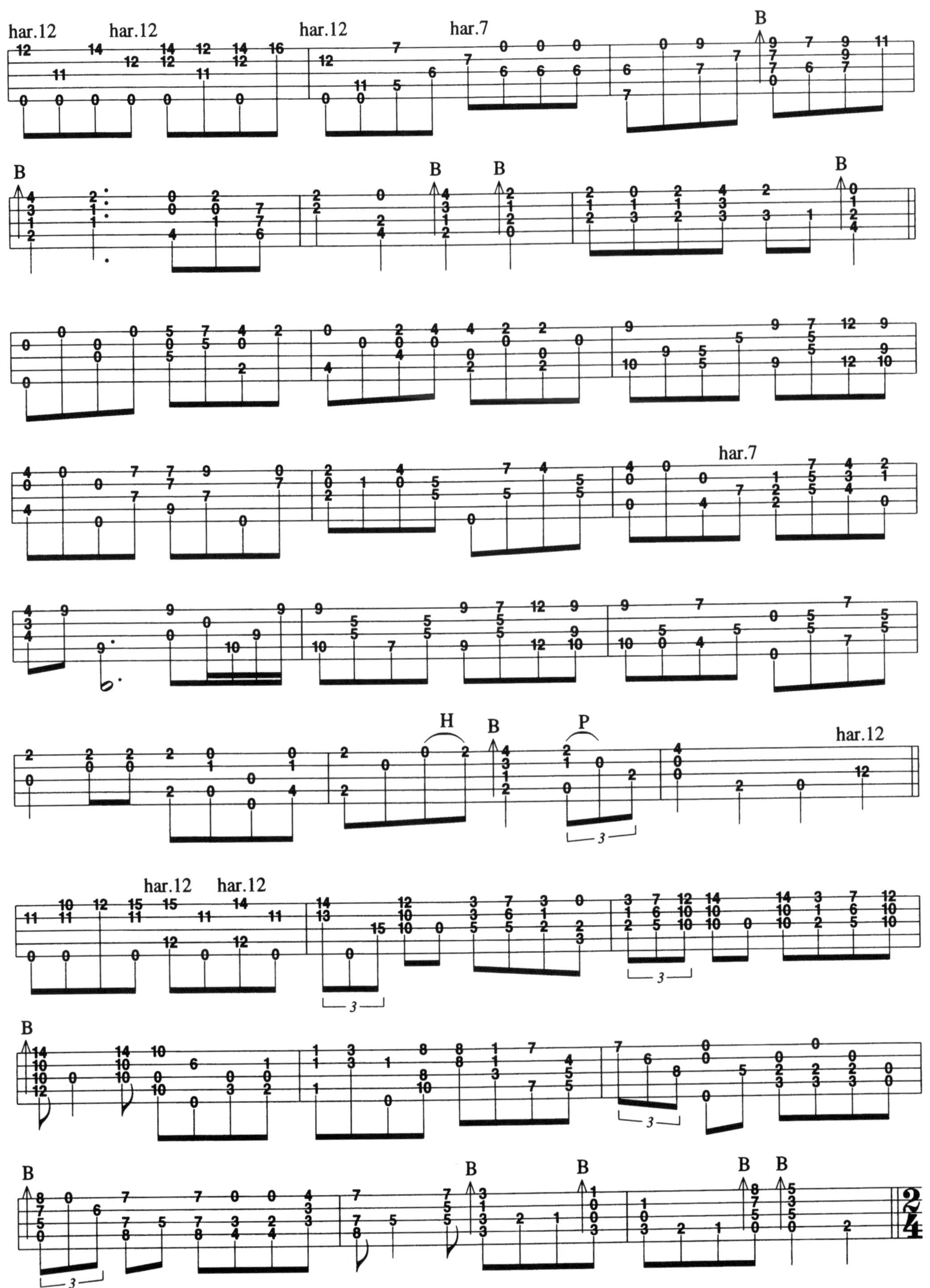
har.12
har.12
har.12
har.7
B
B
B
B
B
har.7
H
B
P
har.12
har.12
har.12
B
B
B
B
B
B
B

har.12
har.12
B
G
G
H
har.12
har.7

SICILIENNE

(from Pelleas et Melisande)

Arranged for banjo
By Larry Vanek
C Tuning

Gabriel Faure

har.12
har.12
H
har.5
har.12
har.17
B
B
B
B
D.S.% al Coda
Coda
har.5
H
har.5
har.17

APPENDIX

Ukrainian Folk Trilogy

The Wide Dnepr River - Traditional

The Bandurist - Traditional

Don't Go, Gregory - Traditional

These three Ukrainian folk songs are arranged for the classical banjo and can be played individually or as a medley. I think they work well as a medley in the order here presented, in which they also progress both in length and degree of difficulty. The "Wide Dnepr River" is the easiest of the three, with "The Bandurist" being somewhat more difficult. "Don't Go, Gregory" is the most difficult of the three, mostly due to its greater length and the rigorous left hand work which it requires. Still, this piece can be played fairly comfortably if it is kept in mind that it should be played at a relatively slow tempo. These three pieces are all in a minor key and their hauntingly beautiful melodies reflect the sense of melancholy characteristically found in much Slavic folk music.

THE WIDE DNEPR RIVER

Arranged for banjo
by Larry Vanek
G Tuning

Traditional Ukrainian
folk song

THE BANDURIST

Arranged for banjo
by Larry Vanek
G Tuning

Traditional Ukrainian
folk song

DON'T GO, GREGORY

Arranged for banjo
by Larry Vanek
G Tuning

Traditional Ukrainian
folk song

Made in the USA
Lexington, KY
15 May 2016